Knowledge, ideology and the politics of schooling

By the same author

with Anthony Green

Education and Social Control. A Study of Progressive Primary Education

Knowledge, ideology and the politics of schooling

Towards a Marxist analysis of education

Rachel Sharp

Routledge & Kegan Paul
London, Boston and Henley

First published in 1980
by Routledge & Kegan Paul Ltd
39 Store Street, London WC1E 7DD
9 Park Street, Boston, Mass. 02108, USA and
Broadway House, Newtown Road,
Henley-on-Thames, Oxon RG9 1EN
Set in IBM Journal 10 on 12pt by
Hope Services, Abingdon, Oxon
and printed in Great Britain by
Lowe & Brydone Ltd
Thetford, Norfolk

British Library Cataloguing in Publication Data

Sharp, Rachel

Knowledge. ideology and the politics of schooling
1. Educational sociology
I. Title
301.5'6   LC189   80 40494

ISBN 0 7100 0526 1
ISBN 0 7100 0527 X Pbk

Dedicated to Patrick White and other Australians
who *will* not see with 'blind blue eyes'

Contents

Introduction

Before I left England I used the term ideology relatively loosely. My deeper interest in the concept dates from my arrival in Australia. For various historical reasons emanating, partly, from its colonial past, and the absence of an old established hegemonic ruling class with distinctive indigenous traditions, the manifestations of bourgeois ideology in Australia seemed to me to be quite dissimilar from their more subtle counterparts in England. Their resistance to what I then thought were rational arguments aroused my interest in the nature of the social practices which sustain an ideology which appeared singularly naked and crude. My first afternoon in the country had been spent wandering around Fremantle, where I saw a prison with immense walls heavily guarded by armed warders. I wondered what kind of society was it that could display a coercive apparatus of the state so blatantly in a peaceful sundrenched suburban setting. I began to think of myself as a Marxist for the first time within two weeks of my arrival.

As is customary with many migrants, the stresses and dislocations are partially managed by identifying strongly with one's country of origin. I yearned for the 'sophistication' of English intellectual life and culture. When I returned there, however, several years later, I was shocked to find that I experienced exactly the same impression concerning the crudity of bourgeois ideology that I had felt on coming to Australia.

I now appreciate that it was my own analysis of the phenomenon which was at fault. Ideology may be insidious, but never crude to those whom it imprisons.

In Sydney, several feminist friends, trying to convert me to the cause, concerning which I had some misgivings, suggested that I was operating from a very simplistic viewpoint. I started to read more deeply in the area and found recent developments in the theory of ideology both provocative and politically important. However, the language of the debate is often impenetrable for those without a background in Marxist theory, or who have only recently begun to appreciate the significance of the concept of ideology.

This book does not pretend to be original. It rather attempts to communicate some of the insights which stimulated me from my reading in a more systematic way in order to show why the analysis of schooling can be invigorated by a theory of ideology. I am heavily indebted to all the authors cited in the bibliography, especially to Liz Jacka, whose Ph.D. thesis used the distinction between practical ideology and theoretical ideology, which I have found very useful.

I wish to express my thanks to Rosemary Pringle and Ann Game who first made me aware of the contribution of feminist theory to the problem, and to male chauvinists everywhere who indirectly, and unwittingly, made me realize the relative imperviousness of ideology when confronted by rational arguments. My failure to realize this has always been a besetting weakness. I owe a debt to some of my students and to the contributors to the *Weekly Guardian*, who sensitized me to the ideological components of everyday language.

Mervyn Hartwig encouraged me to write the book at some crucial moments of self-doubt and explored with me many of the themes. He also stressed the interrelationship between subtle precision of thought and literary style, although I am fully conscious that despite great effort, the style (and presumably the thought) could be improved. I am grateful for his and Vic Sharp's refusal to be 'white liberals' which is essential if reason is to penetrate ideology, although I am aware that I have not provided all the answers.

I thank my colleagues at Macquarie University for their encouragement, especially Ken Johnston, who first introduced me to some of the recent work on the history of class struggles over education which provided an inspiration; Ian O'Farrell, who continually reminded me that I have important things to say despite my 'sweeping statements and unsupported comments', and Jim Alexander, who carefully went through the manuscript and made many constructive suggestions, some of which I, unfortunately, had to ignore.

I am grateful to Muriel Keogh, Claire Weller and Judy Faulkner, who valiantly struggled with a handwritten and messy manuscript and corrected my spelling and punctuation with assiduous care.

Finally, I thank Daniel, David, Hannah, Lizzie and Leonie for their cheerful resignation in the face of what can only be described as rampant neglect whilst the book was being written. The final responsibility for its contents rests with me.

1 Liberal theory and the crisis in bourgeois society

Western industrial nations in the post-war period have experienced two conflicting trends: an almost unprecedented expansion of the productive forces and an increase in the rate of capital accumulation; followed by a serious decline in the level of economic activity and the onset of a cyclical depression unparalleled since the 1930s.

The phase of expansion was characterized by a recovery of optimism and self-confidence within bourgeois society. After the major crises of the twentieth century – two world wars, the Russian Revolution, an economic depression which almost disrupted the capitalist economic system, the rise of fascism in Germany and Italy – the 1950s provided a welcome reminder of the ability of the capitalist system to fulfil its promises. Mandel has called this period the Third Technological Revolution (Mandel, 1975). The decade was one of full employment and rising real wages in most western countries, helped, no doubt, by state intervention in the economy, based on Keynesian assumptions. These factors facilitated the ideological incorporation of subordinate classes and a temporary demise in the traditional pattern of overt class politics. Internationally, the colonial empires of the west were rapidly being dismantled in such a way as to safeguard western neocolonial interests. The achievement of political independence by the colonies posed little substantive threat to those social relations of domination which secured for the metropolitan bourgeoisie, through the collaboration of ruling strata in the periphery, effective control over the allocation and utilization of productive resources.

This was the era of the end of ideology thesis (Bell, 1960), the faith in the redistributory potential of the welfare state, a commitment to and belief in the possibility of 'modernizing' the 'third world', the end of the cold war and the onset of international coexistence. Class divisions seemed to be giving way to an emerging middle-class homogeneity.

By the middle of the 1960s, however, a more pessimistic outlook

1

was developing with the appearance of the symptoms of a crisis in the western world. In the social formations of the periphery, the most sensitive barometer of bourgeois class rule, democratically elected constitutional governments, often with a populist flavour and mass social basis, were being replaced, one by one, by various types of authoritarian regime, whilst in the metropolitan centres, in the advanced capitalist countries themselves, the ideological appurtenances of bourgeois class rule seemed vulnerable to an open discontent. The coercive apparatuses of the state, the ultimate guarantor of class domination were becoming more visible, thus signalling a potential crisis of hegemony.

Against such a background, it is hardly surprising that sociology has undergone some major shifts in orientation. Whilst some developments within social theory must be explained partly in terms of the working out of the inner logic of the ideas themselves, such changes have to be related to the subtle interplay between ideas and the context and conditions within which they are generated. The post-war period has seen the rise and subsequent partial demise of what Gouldner has called Parsonian structural-functionalism (Gouldner, 1970); the development of various strands of conflict theory which focus attention on the inadequacy of such theory for dealing with problems of conflict and structural change; and the emergence of idealist social psychologies in symbolic interactionism, phenomenology and ethnomethodology. The latter are often associated with a retreat into epistemological relativism. The period has also witnessed a partial incorporation of some Marxian concepts into the abstract formalism of French structuralism.

Despite a pretence that sociology provides explanations of social phenomena in the 'real world', most of the liveliest discussions in the discipline in recent years have been concerned with meta-questions concerning ontology, epistemology or methodology. Issues of substance surrounding the interpretation of current social changes have been neglected. Unlike Weber, Durkheim, Michels or Veblen, few sociologists would now venture to offer authoritative statements about the causes of significant national or international social developments.

These strands and tendencies within sociology, it is suggested, are indicative of a bourgeois class on the defensive, affected by the inner antinomies of bourgeois theory and its vulnerability in the face of historical changes which are difficult to incorporate without tension within the structure of liberal thought. Although some may have gained security by a retreat into self-conscious solipsism, another phenomenon of significance has been occurring: the resurgence of

Marxist scholarship after the aridity and petrifaction of the Stalinist period. It must be remembered that classical sociology developed at least partly in response to the assault by Marxism, not simply on the underlying assumptions of bourgeois theory, but on the nature of bourgeois society itself. Without in any way invoking an idealist explanation of the political failure of Marxism *vis à vis* social democracy and reformism in the last one hundred years in western industrial societies, the significance of the contribution of bourgeois sociology to a reconstituted ideological hegemony cannot be denied.

The wheel has now turned full circle. Again the bourgeois class is faced with the growth of a counter-hegemonic challenge of some importance in which the emergence of a reinvigorated Marxist tradition in the social sciences is by no means an insignificant element. However, bougeois sociology is now less well equipped organizationally to withstand the challenge emanating from Marxism than hitherto. Since the time of its classical founders, a division of labour has developed between the high priests of theory and those concerned with data collection and analysis. This trend has been associated by an ever-expanding multiplication of the internal boundaries between disciplines and subdisciplines, all part of the increasing specialization of intellectual work which has been steadily in process throughout the twentieth century. In place of the grand classical theorists (Weber, Durkheim, Simmel, Pareto and others), the discipline is now manned by a large contigent of professionalized guardians of highly esoteric, specialized, but often ultimately trivial knowledge, who do not share a universalizing world view which has the potential for transcending the level of common sense. Preoccupied with regularities and complexity perceived on the surface of the social world, and utilizing theoretical models which focus on the level of appearances, itself encapsulated by bourgeois thought, modern sociologists are frequently incapable of explaining any of the underlying determinants of these surface manifestations. This process has, moreover, been accentuated by the increasing professionalization of social scientists and by their incorporation into government and other public and private bureaucracies, thus signalling the demise of the independent scholar who actively sought to distance himself from his own society in order to safeguard at least some of the preconditions for objectivity. Society is thus faced with the paradox that, despite a huge growth in the number of 'experts' on social life, frequently financed or employed by the state either directly or within universities, the conditions for genuine knowledge are extremely precarious.

3

It will be argued in this book that one of the first principles in the search for knowledge involves a recognition that those whose business it is to provide an 'expert', i.e. an 'objective' and 'impartial' authoritative commentary on the social world's events are frequently important purveyors of theoretical ideology. It is necessary to demystify expertise. What is invoked by the concept of ideology will be elaborated in more detail below. Nevertheless, at this stage it is important to show the differences between a Marxist concept of ideology and a notion of bias. The suggestion is not that society's experts are biased. Such a concept has a place only in an essentially liberal world view. The liberal acknowledges the existence of many different points of view, some perfectly legitimate, but others involving distortion derived from the intrusion of a particular political or moral position, the grounds for which are ultimately arbitrary. For the liberal, the search for knowledge entails the avoidance of bias and the pursuit of truth. The latter lies either somewhere in between (the liberal will nowadays rarely speak with confidence concerning where he believes the truth resides) or it resides nowhere, which is the position of epistemological relativism. In contrast, the concept of ideology in Marxist theory refers not simply to the level of ideas but to the whole range of social practices which reproduce and transfigure in ideological form the social relationships of production, which, in class societies, are social relationships of domination. Thus the varying 'points of view' of which bourgeois theory speaks are themselves different manifestations of ideology. So is the assumption that the truth lies somewhere in between through the avoidance of bias. It is significant that it is only potentially counter-hegemonic 'points of view', whether emanating from the right or from the left, which are usually characterized as biased by the liberal. In the same way that the respectable liberal political position is in the middle ground of social democratic politics, so epistemologically the best position is in the avoidance of extremes. How reassuring to be able to invoke the Greek doctrine of the mean on one's side.

This crisis in sociology concerning what constitutes knowledge of society is reproduced within the sociology of education perhaps in an even more acute form because of its historically marginal position both intellectually and organizationally, with respect to the mainstream. The discipline has also been more affected than other specialist areas by the process of incorporation whereby the problems of the discipline are defined in terms of the preoccupations of the policy-makers, those whose business is to finance, manage, and shape the form and content of the institutional order through which education takes place, or who are required to act within education as administrators, teachers or curriculum advisers. The post-war period has seen a vast increase in the number of sociologists of education employed directly or indirectly by government agencies or by organizations like the N.F.E.R. and the Schools Council, as policy advisers or as research workers. Inevitably this trend has tended to be reflected in the key underlying assumption of the discipline: what is at issue is the improvement of education within a basically social democratic system. Solutions are prescribed within this framework, which is not, in any fundamental way, exposed to critical examination.

Parallel with the trend towards incorporation has been the increasing isolation of the discipline from other areas within the social sciences which might be thought to be central to a full understanding of how educational systems function: from history, economics, politics and anthropology, on the one hand, and from psychology and physiology on the other. Moreover, within the sociology of education itself a whole series of subspecializations have emerged which tend to have some degree of autonomy of their own. Instead of a unified sociology of education, we now have macro-sociological approaches to education, a sociology of the school, sociology of the curriculum, sociology of the classroom, sociology of learning, sociology of higher education, sociology of childhood, sociology of youth, and so on, together with numerous fields of study which are in some way related: sociology of language, of the media, of deviance, of literature, of culture, of the family, of stratification, comparative sociology – the list goes on. The central theoretical and substantive problems are dissipated through an ever-increasing fragmentation into their alleged component parts around which professional experts cluster with their vested interests in defining educational problems in 'their own, often ultimately trivial, terms. Despite a claim that such specialization can assist in the elaboration of a theoretical system of some complexity and rigour, the more likely consequence is a retreat into empiricism, the collection of a mass of data and its analysis in terms of low-level hypotheses which ultimately do little more than reproduce a more articulated version of common sense.

The sociology of education thus suffers from incorporation, fragmentation, and empiricism. In the late 1960s however, there arose some lively debates associated with the emergence of what some have called the New Sociology of Education, which developed arguments, deriving from what was earlier described as conflict theory, against

5

what was rightly regarded as the dominant tradition in the sociology of education, structural-functionalism. A new orientation for research was proposed which would utilize some of the key insights of symbolic interactionism, phenomenology and ethnomethodology.

The criticisms of structural-functionalism are manifold. It presupposes the functionality and historical necessity of stratification in societies generally, and in complex industrial societies in particular (Davis and Moore, 1966). The idea of the inevitability of the social division of labour being associated with differences in power, economic rewards and social status is rarely questioned. Instead, the preoccupation becomes the role of education in social selection and in particular how to ensure the institutionalization of equality of opportunity, i.e. the free movement of individuals within a hierarchical structure according to talent and motivation, as opposed to ascriptive criteria more characteristic of an earlier age.

In structural functionalism there is basically a cultural explanation of social transformation. Industrial societies are constantly undergoing change as science and its application to technology produces further differentiation in the division of labour leading to greater complexity in the stratification system.

Educational systems are seen as institutions which gradually adapt themselves to these technological and social imperatives. Of course all institutions suffer from some degree of structural inertia, there are cultural lags or structural disequilibria – but gradually the inner tendency towards a re-established equilibrium operates.

Much structural-functionalist research into education revolved around the identification of these cultural and structural lags. That which focused attention on the educational effects of the 1944 Education Act, for example, was informed not by any underlying assumption that educational equality of opportunity was in principle impossible without a fundamental transformation of the system, but by a belief that through identifying the biases built into the educational system and shedding more light upon them, more progressive policies could ensue. Thus, the demonstration among other things, of the cultural deprivation, for example, of working-class pupils compared with their middle-class counterparts led to practical solutions aimed at the cultural resocialization of disadvantaged pupils to provide them with greater opportunities (Riessman, 1962). Such policies were advocated alongside other social reforms concerning redistribution of incomes and resources into areas so deprived.

As Finn, Grant and Johnson (1977) have suggested, the sociology of education in Britain in the first two decades after the war developed within a Fabian, social reformist social and political theory. Implicit in the approach was a theory of the social democratic state, as the rational directing centre of society, the main means whereby, through growing knowledge and social awareness, more informed social policies could be implemented.

The developing critique of these assumptions, of course, cannot be explained in purely idealist terms as resulting from a progression in their own internal logic. If the post-war boom had continued to provide full employment, rising real standards of living and a continued expansion of the welfare state, it is likely that structural-functionalism would still be the dominant paradigm. However, these conditions, as has been seen, did not obtain: the growing contradictions of capitalist production at the international level and the ongoing structural crises of British capitalism in particular, generated the conditions for the inner tensions within the dominant mode of bourgeois social theory to become manifest. The ensuing crisis resulted in the development of a rigorous intellectual critique.

It was the contribution of the New Sociologists of Education to bring these tensions out into the open. From the mid 1960s onwards, a series of critical attacks were made on the epistemological, methodological and ontological assumptions of the older approach. These had wide-ranging implications for breaking down what had been a powerful consensus regarding what should be the significant substantive concerns of the discipline and how they should be theorized and explored (Young, 1971b).

Apart from the systematic exposé of the political and social value judgments built into the structural functionalist perspective, the main contention of the New Sociology of Education was that the central issue should be the question of educational knowledge (Davies, 1971). It was suggested, with some exaggeration, that the earlier tradition has tended to take the question of the content of knowledge for granted, whereas in reality educational knowledge involves a series of conscious and unconscious choices. An educational curriculum can only ever be a *selection*. It was thus incumbent upon the researcher to explore the range of cultural meanings and typifications of those involved in the process of educational transmission, because it is through a dynamic process of negotiation that their notions of education, differentiated pupil types and definitions of worthwhile knowledge are socially

7

constructed. Whereas structural-functionalism has tended to treat schools as passive filters, which process pupils with different prior socialization and hence varying educational potential, the new sociology resulted in a refocusing of attention towards the cultural differentiations of pupils and of knowledge within the school itself. At the heart of the new perspective lay the belief that the process of social reproduction was none other than a process of cultural reproduction. Educational inequality was seen to emanate primarily from the cultural practices and typifications within the context of the school, whilst social inequality at the societal level became a matter of social definition and the 'routine accomplishments' of members as they went about their daily lives.

This approach will be examined in more detail in Chapter 3 in the context of a discussion of Michael Young's work. For the present it is important to see that in spite of the sometimes ferocious nature of the debate between the old and the new sociologists of education, concerning their alleged incompatibility, in a number of important respects a fundamental continuity unites them. Bernbaum has put forward a similar thesis, but from the perspective of someone who himself thinks of education from within the confines of liberal (albeit left liberal) social assumptions which are precisely what needs to be criticized (Bernbaum, 1977).

Despite their apparent radicalism, the New Sociologists of Education are still encapsulated within the parameters of liberal thought about society, schooling and social action. Never engaging in any systematic critique of their own essentially ahistorical and voluntarist premises, and generally unself-conscious concerning the structural context within which their own thought is evolving, they portray the cultural determination of social structures and the structural primacy of consciousness, which is precisely what liberal thought would have us believe. Relying on an essentialist notion of human nature, like the structural functionalists they criticize, they provide support for the view that through greater self-consciousness and awareness cultural meanings can be transformed and the social structure thereby regenerated along new lines. Moreover, although they oppose a positivistic methodology and the use of quantitative techniques and data analysis, their own methodological prescriptions are as empiricist as the methodology they criticize. The suspension of all preconceptions, the phenomenological reduction, is, of course, an epistemological impossibility. The investigation of the raw data of cultural meanings unmediated by any arbitrary theoretical constructs entails a positivistic premise that the goal of sociology is to describe and analyse the world as it really is, albeit a socially constructed and negotiated one. Moreover, in the same way that the structural functionalists 'took' the problems of policy-makers as their own rather than made them (Seeley, 1966), so the new preoccupations were tied in with those of teachers, trainee teachers and others interested in the practical problems of what happens within the four walls of the classroom.

Both the New Sociology of Education and, to a lesser extent, structural-functionalism, operate with the key, quite incorrect and fundamentally liberal assumption that one can grasp the workings of the educational system by centring the analysis on *its* inner processes. It is the contention of the author that such a view reinforces the fetishized nature of social relations within capitalist society which obscures the structural primacy of production relations. The analysis of the processes of what are, in fact, bourgeois educational systems, depends upon a theoretical constitution of the object – 'bourgeois society'. Without such a theoretically constructed analysis, the inner workings of the educational system will remain hidden. Despite the prescription to investigate the taken-for-granted assumptions within everyday life, the new sociologists of education do not examine their own key assumption, that cultural meanings and the 'taken-for-granted' (Schutz, 1943), is the key to understanding social reality.

It is the theme of this book that a central element of a theory of education is a theory of ideology: that a deeper structural reality exists below that encapsulated in consciousness and ideological forms. In Chapter 4, what a theory of ideology entails and its significance for education will be outlined. Neither structural-functionalism nor the new sociology, however, utilizes a concept of ideology. Their analyses and conclusions suffer as a consequence.

Earlier it was suggested that the processes of specialization, fragmentation and incorporation of the social sciences are indicative of a fundamental crisis in bourgeois society and of the ideological legitimation of this crisis in bourgeois social theory. Whilst the new sociologists of education have identified the question of the management and social construction of knowledge within education as the most critical substantive issue, given its significance for the social 'construction of reality', they provide us with no concepts to analyse the social reproduction process except those which are ultimately tautological. An adequate theory of cultural meanings, or cultural reproduction, involves an analysis of the interrelationship between culture and that which is not culture. Specialization within the social sciences renders such questions incapable of resolution. Marxism, on the other hand, provides a set of theoretical categories which can elucidate significant social interconnections and transcend the arbitrary division of the social world into a range of discrete subject areas which produce little more than specialized myopia. Such concepts as 'mode of production' and 'social formation' provide a basis for understanding the inner structure and dynamics of different societies. They also provide a framework within which to analyse education both historically and comparatively at any one point in time. Bernbaum argues, by contrast, for an approach to educational knowledge which locates educational knowledge within a context of 'industrialization' and 'changes in social stratification' (1977, p. 65) without providing any concepts for the comprehension of such a context. A *sine qua non* of an adequate problematic involves relinquishing the framework of bourgeois social thought concerning education and society. What needs to be developed is a holistic conceptual structure which may have little readily apparent relation to what bourgeois social theorists believe should be explained. Those who wish to understand education should, if necessary, forget about it for a number of years and concentrate their attention instead on more significant issues concerning the nature and dynamics of capitalist societies. Such a project necessitates, at least initially, the suspension of one's specialized identity as a sociologist of education, for only thus can one begin to penetrate the fetishized nature of bourgeois social relations and the ideological content of bourgeois social thought.

2 Education and the classical sociological tradition

In this chapter the work of four social theorists will be examined. Veblen, Weber and Durkheim were all contemporaries whilst Mannheim was some thirty years younger. Each wrote interestingly on the subject of education and all are regarded as influencing in some vital way the direction of the sociology of education generally and the study of the content of schooling in particular. Yet they were in no way narrow specialists. All thought it important to situate the analysis of education within a broader holistic framework in order to facilitate a more comprehensive theory.

The theme in this chapter will be the specific manner in which each tried to come to terms with the analysis of capitalist industrialization, its characteristic trends and implications for education, and the remedies they offered for the social ills of their time. The argument will centre on the extent to which they were all, in their different ways, in some measure, prisoners of certain basic liberal assumptions about capitalism in general and education in particular. With the partial exception of Veblen, none of them operated with a sufficiently rigorous concept of either capitalism as a dynamic mode of production or of ideology. In both this and the subsequent chapter, the consequence of this theoretical deficiency for developing a theory of education in capitalist society will be elaborated.

Thorstein Veblen

It is not as an authority on education, nor as a sociologist and economist of international stature, that Veblen is best remembered, but as America's most brilliant social critic whose incisive exposé of the leisured classes and their pecuniary values has left a legacy of graphic phrases which devastatingly penetrate a form of social life whose premises he both hated and wished to expose.

Whilst embarking originally on a course of higher education to prepare him for the vocation of a Lutheran pastor, Veblen soon became an agnostic and transferred his intellectual interests to the social sciences, in particular to economics. He developed a critique of the ahistorical assumptions of classical economics and the hedonistic model of man built into utilitarian theory. In place of utilitarianism, he advocated a version of social evolutionary theory, which committed him to a view of the essentially transitory nature of any particular set of social institutions, given the transformations entailed in their long-term selective adaptation to the environment. Nevertheless, he made no claim to dissect history and produce a detailed analysis of historical change. On the contrary, his primary concern was to grasp the essential features of his own society and elucidate its inner dynamics; not in order to demonstrate where things were leading – for, indeed, history leads nowhere, it has no goal – but rather to characterize the nature of the social context within which modern man has to function, to satirize and poke fun at its most dehumanizing and hateful features, to vent his spleen upon it in the hope that people would be able to see it more clearly for what it was.

The key to his analysis lies in the notion of a basic contradiction between what he calls business production, which is controlled by pecuniary classes who live by and off economic activities which are organized for private profit and pecuniary gain, and industry, which is production motivated by the desire to satisfy human needs in an efficient, rational manner, based upon man's inborn instinct of workmanship, his ability and desire to provide himself with an efficient technology and the natural satisfaction to be derived from useful hard work and self-discipline (Veblen, 1935).

The pecuniary classes, according to Veblen, are opposed to true industry. They owe their origin, historically, to the development of a surplus sufficient to support a class of non-workers, and to the exercise of predatory instincts through such processes as military conquest, the institutionalization of private property and the subordination of females to males. Their contemporary counterparts are the leisured classes who owe their existence partly to the institution of private property, which facilitates absentee ownership, and, more importantly, to the creation of banking and other credit-generating institutions necessary for the development of the large-scale and expensive machine-based technology characteristic of the modern era (Veblen, 1970).

Veblen diagnoses modern industrial production as subordinated to the essentially parasitic goals of the pecuniary, or business, classes – the captains of industry, the vested interests. In any long-term historical sense, they retard industrial progress. They, not the industrial workers, are the originators of industrial sabotage. Their operations produce, within the anarchy of the market place, the various cyclical upturns and downturns in the industrial business cycle, causing a fundamental disequilibrium between the amount of products produced and people's ability to consume, and between the type and quantity of production and the satisfaction of social needs. Veblen shows how pecuniary motives lead to advertising, conspicuous waste, the unproductive utilization or under-utilization of human labour and other resources in the service of nothing more than private profit-making, whilst the potential offered by advancing technology cannot be harnessed within the present organization of production. Far from satisfying human needs, the hold of the pecuniary classes over important decision-making processes produces private affluence amid a wider context of unproductive waste. Veblen is very optimistic about history in the long run, but is very pessimistic in the short run. Although technological progress will eventually require a dissolution of the pecuniary classes and their institutions because they retard the evolutionary process, in the meantime, they are seen to possess enormous power over the social processes of everyday life. Whilst castigating them for their decadence and parasitic existence, their institutionalized wastefulness through 'conspicuous consumption' and for their leisure activities, Veblen recognizes that their habits of living and cognitive style thoroughly permeate society. They encourage a rat race of status-striving and emulation, given the tendency, which is socially contrived, for people to fear a loss of self-esteem. The culture of the leisured classes thus infects the whole society. Their habits of living produce a common-sense consciousness which becomes the world view of the epoch. Their influence is felt throughout all social institutions in civil society and in the state. Veblen develops a theory of the latter, for example, which views it as an instrument for enhancing business profitability. His analysis of international military competition is couched in similar terms. (See, for example, his brilliant discussion of the First World War in his book on imperial Germany (Veblen, 1964).)

In the context of the conflict between the pecuniary and industrial classes, those who produce cash and those who produce goods, Veblen develops an analysis of educational institutions as one of the sites of contradictory social pressures and influences. He sees the function of education for the children of the industrial classes as concerned with their socialization into the attitudes and skills necessitated by the requirements of work roles, whereas its function for the leisured classes, in higher learning, is initiation into a status-differentiating culture with its symbolism and rituals generated by its leisured life-style (Veblen, 1969). However, he identifies important changes occurring in the higher learning. Whereas in the past universities had facilitated, at least for some, the pursuit of idle curiosity, the encouragement of intellectual values and disinterested learning, increasingly they are being taken over by the captains of industry, with business interests and preoccupations shaping not merely the content of education and pedagogy, but the very mode of organizing, administering and financing educational institutions. What had once been relatively autonomous seats of learning are now being subjected to powerful external pressures, to the detriment of scholarly values and intellectual activity.

In the face of such tendencies, Veblen rejected any romantic con-servative retreat to some halcyon past. A good evolutionist could only believe that history moves forward, albeit to no goal. Veblen had been influenced by Edward Bellamy, the author of a utopian novel called *Looking Backwards* (1888): an influential socialist of a populist variety, who had projected a model of a planned, rational society in which the state had abolished private property and in which production was for the public good. Nevertheless, whilst remaining an inveterate opponent of the institution of private property, Veblen was not optimistic that its days were numbered, least of all in America. He applauded the Russian Revolution and at least conceived the *possibility* of a soviet of engineers organizing production even in his own country, but he did not deem it likely, even though he regarded private property as inherently inimical to the interests of the common people (Veblen, 1965).

It is clear from the foregoing that Veblen operates with an implicit theory of ideology, which, although lacking in clarity and rigour, accounts for the fact that most people are unable or unwilling to see through the activities of vested interests and are thus victims of clever political manoeuvres. He identifies engineers and technological experts as the critical class for any revolutionary transformation. It is on them that absentee owners and the pecuniary classes rely for the efficient organization of profit-making and hence for the basis of their wealth and social position. All that is required is for them to simply open their eyes and see the system they are enclosed in for what it is, and to organize with other key workers in transport and basic industry to delegitimate and hence disarm the absentee captains of industry whose priorities they have hitherto slavishly and unthinkingly followed. However, Veblen hastens to add that the vested interests have little to fear from 'red Bolshevism':

> By settled habit the technicians, and the engineers and industrial experts are a harmless and docile sort, well fed on the whole and somewhat placidly content with the 'full dinner pail' which the lieutenants of the vested interests habitually allow them. . . They have hitherto been quite unreflectingly content to work piecemeal without much of an understanding among themselves, unreservedly doing jobwork for the Vested Interest; and they have without much reflection lent themselves and their technical powers freely to the destructive tactics of the captains of industry. (1965, p. 135)

Unlike proponents of the two main tendencies in recent sociology, empiricism and formalistic grand theorizing, Veblen attempted to 'grasp the essentials of an entire society and epoch, to delineate the characters of the typical men within it, to determine its main drift' (Mills, 1953). Eschewing narrow professionalism or specialization, well-read in history, economics, philosophy, psychology and sociology, he tried to elucidate the moral, psychological and cultural implications of the domination of social life by business values towards which he felt a profound revulsion. It is precisely the clarity with which he sees the system for what it is, that prevents him from advocating easy recourse to any simplistic social engineering, remedies designed to gloss over or mask what to Veblen were irremediable defects. For example, in respect of higher learning he proposes an unrealistic, total abolition of the academic executive and governing bodies of the universities, for 'anything short of this heroic remedy is bound to fail, because the evils sought to be remedied are inherent in these organs and intrinsic to their functioning.'

However, in spite of the devastating nature of Veblen's moral critique there is a certain superficiality in his analysis of why things are as they are. Although recognizing the significance of the pecuniary classes in determining so much of what occurs in social life, he fails to show how it is the inner logic of the market rather than capitalist greed or financial profiteering which produces the phenomena he castigates. He seemed to have been familiar with some aspects of Marxism, but Adorno suggests that it is mainly the secondary aspects of Marxism that he incorporated into what was essentially a pragmatist position (Adorno, 1967). He was sympathetic to Marx's moral critique of capitalism in the name of socialist objectives, but he never grasped the potential of Marx's analysis of political economy, nor did he conceptualize capitalism as an inherently expansionist mode of production operating in terms of an inherent logic based on the objective movement of the law of value. His analysis is framed more in terms of populist categories which never manage to break completely with the dominant assumptions of hegemonic thought. For example, closer to Hobson than to Marx, Veblen's theory of history ultimately seems to degenerate into a form of technological determinism. He does not analyse technology or machine-processes in the context of the primacy of social relations of production which ultimately determine the form which technology takes. Similarly, although he opposes the tendency within bourgeois thought to eternize the nature of capitalism, he is hardly optimistic about the possibility that it can be transformed. He has an almost Nietzschean pessimism, resembling that of the later Carlyle concerning the ability or desire of the industrial classes, the ordinary people, ever to do anything other than acquiesce in the conditions of their dehumanization. He has no coherent political programme to offer; his role is a social critic's: 'we are interested in what is, not in what ought to be' (quoted in Dorfman, 1966). This is an apt self-characterization, not in the sense that Veblen shies away from a moral condemnation of what is, but that he neglects the key political question as to how to transcend that which morally has to be eschewed. Indeed, one of the key concepts in his theory, emanating from its social evolutionary assumptions, is that of adjustment. He fails to grasp that: 'adjustment to what is possible no longer means adjustment; it means making the possible real' (Adorno, 1967).

Veblen's pessimism is also revealed in his discussion of the relation of the leisured class to art. Whilst observing the negative and deforming aspects of aesthetic experience, he never seems to penetrate the positive potential of art in simultaneously encapsulating the contradictory aspects of social life whilst projecting a way beyond them. This contempt for the aesthetic is characterized by the way he 'idolizes the sphere of production', reflecting a view of the inevitability of scarcity and a continual struggle for human existence based upon material need (Adorno, 1967). Marxism, of course, is not a theory of scarcity. If there is scarcity in class societies, it is the result of the social division of labour and the private appropriation of the surplus product. The advances in the forces of production, especially under capitalism, create the preconditions for the overcoming of scarcity, the disappearance of the dichotomy between the useful and the useless, and the possibility of all human life becoming an art form.

These weaknesses in his theory can possibly be explained by turning Veblen's own analysis of the power of ideology back on to his own work. Although he did not himself use the concept, he recognized, as has been seen, the importance of habits and social routines in generating and moulding particular cognitive styles and contents; he saw the importance of class position and material interests in the moulding of world views, and helped to identify the specific ways in which, through institutions like education and the mass media, such ideologies were transmitted and consolidated. His theory, however, lacks any access to the critical question concerning how an escape from ideology might be possible.

Veblen's life and work provides testimony to the positive and negative effects of marginality. Always to some extent on the 'outside', he could see some of the features of his social context with brilliant clarity. However, social marginality tends to lead to an ambivalent relationship to the dominant culture. Lacking any structural support for his social criticism, he was still partly trapped within the ideology of his time. A full appraisal of his thought would locate it within the context of American history from the 1880s to 1920s, an era in which a major structural reorganization of capitalist production, a heightening of class struggles and increasing international competition occurred. Such disturbances provided the basis for the development of a potential counter-hegemonic consciousness, albeit with strong petit bourgeois components, as well as the occasion for a reconstitution of the dominant hegemony by the bourgeois class. This was carried out with the assistance of the state incorporating the populist and socialist movements in such a way as to isolate and render impotent their more radical elements. Veblen's work thus raises a question of key theoretical and potential significance: how to produce the ability to penetrate the structure of hegemonic meanings, how to capitalize on a psychological sense of marginality and alienation from the dominant ideology, whilst simultaneously avoiding the pitfalls of pessimism, fatalism or cynicism, on the one hand, or of a retreat into a romantic, profoundly conservative and ultimately reactionary position, on the other. Both tendencies are consequences of a fundamentally petit bourgeois class position. Isolated organizationally from any mass social movement, and retaining some of the motivating assumptions derived from his rural and religious Norwegian peasant background, Veblen could not but fail to provide

adequate answers to the important questions that he posed. Nevertheless, the scope of those questions and his sensitivity to the profoundly
injurious consequences of the profit motive, together with his refusal
to define himself as a servant of social engineering, render him a theorist
still worth studying. His brilliantly ironic insights have a lasting currency.

If Veblen's work suffers, in spite of its emotional and moral hostility
to capitalism, from being enclosed within petit bourgeois blinkers,
what of a theorist who unashamedly articulated the world view of the
bourgeois class?

Max Weber

To understand fully Weber's contribution to the analysis of modern
society generally and education in particular, it is necessary to locate
him in the context of post-Bismarckian Germany. The last half of the
nineteenth century had seen the rapid growth of urbanization due to
the expansion of capitalism and its transition to monopoly capitalism,
with the state often deliberately fostering the centralization and concentration of capital. It had also seen the reunification of Germany
under the hegemony of the quasi-feudal Prussian Junker class. Reunification, however, did not prevent a period of political and military
instability in central Europe due to the fact that Germany was now
surrounded by three national empires which seemed to threaten her
territorial integrity.

Weber regarded himself proudly as a German nationalist and as a
spokesman for the bourgeois class. In his view German reunification
had failed to bring about a proper bourgeois revolution at the politcal
level. Although admiring Bismarck for his charismatic qualities, he
lamented what he saw as Bismarck's legacy: a general lack of political
education on the part of the monarchy and the ruling class. Instead
of the German state being controlled by the army, anachronistic
feudal elements and an over-powerful civilian bureaucracy accustomed
to authoritarian rule, Weber wanted to see the bourgeois class acquire
effective political dominance, as, in his view, it had done in England
and America. An ardent nationalist, an admirer of Machiavelli, and an
apologist for 'realpolitik', he did not oppose German imperialist expan-
sionism, often writing in glowing terms about the euphoric experience
of the First World War. He opposed the terms of the Versailles treaty
for nationalistic reasons, and developed a theory of politics which was
analytically separable from issues of morality (Giddens, 1974).

Closely associated with both his nationalism and his class preoccupations was his anti-Marxism. The central themes of his social analysis can be seen as the result of an engagement with the Marxist intellectual tradition which he regarded as intellectually misleading and politically dangerous. The German Social Democratic Party, outlawed under Bismarck, had been legalized in 1890, bringing almost as many candidates into the Reichstag as the National Liberal Party had (Mayer, 1956). The 'harmony of the classes' seemed endangered, especially as the Socialists had been influenced heavily by Marxism and were sceptical of the possibility of achieving their aims of social justice within the framework of the constitutional state and of capitalism. Weber had little faith in the intellectual and political abilities of the masses. Elitist at heart, he was far more preoccupied with domination and leadership than with such issues as democratization, mass participation or social justice.

Weber's opposition to Marxism has been of seminal importance for the development of social theory. He laid the foundation for a theory of stratification, power and historical change which is antithetical both to historical materialism and to political optimism (Stedman Jones, 1976). Whilst appearing to debate with Marx on the latter's own ground – the theoretical analysis of capitalism – although acknowledging the supreme heuristic potential of the hypothesis of economic determination and of class struggle in history, he nevertheless opposed Marxism for its alleged economic determinism and reductionism, for its neglect of the independent role of ideas in historical causation and for its utopianism, which he regarded as irrational, given his views on the ultimately arbitrary and subjectivist nature of individual moral choices (Weber, 1949).

Weber's knowledge of Marx's writings, apart from *The Communist Manifesto*, seems to have been derived largely from secondary sources, from commentators like Kautsky, Sombart and Bernstein. Marx's philosophical works were, of course, unknown to him or to anyone else, for they were only published long after he died. He was by no means alone in thinking of Marxism as a mechanistic account of historical change. Indeed by the time of the Second International even many self-confessed Marxists had lost the dialectical character of Marx's thought, reducing it to an arid positivism. Nevertheless, Weber had little incentive to ensure that his characterization of Marx's work was entirely accurate. From a political point of view, any threat to social hegemony presented by an organized working-class politics was likely to be inspired by Marxist analysis, and much of his work has to be seen as an attempt by a bourgeois intellectual to counteract its effects.

From Weber's immensely erudite writings, the product not simply of a brilliant mind but also outstanding application to the discipline of work (inner-worldly ascetism?) the theme selected for attention will be his diagnosis of the state of contemporary societies, their historical genesis and inner tendencies. It has been suggested (Mayer, 1956) that for all Weber's interest in comparative historical work, his central preoccupation was with trying to understand the reasons for the distinctiveness of western societies and their most salient characteristic: the rationalization process in social life which accompanies the emergence and expansion of capitalism. Agreeing with Marx on what is meant by capitalism – a mode of production based upon private entrepreneurial profit-seeking, utilizing formally free labour from whom the means of production had been appropriated – Weber attempted to locate its genesis in the emergence of the protestant ethic, specifically Calvinism. The latter was a form of inner-worldly asceticism which produced the idea of 'the calling' (Weber, 1967). This entailed a devotion to hard work, self-discipline and material self-denial, which now 'prowls about us like the ghost of some dead religious belief'. Weber sees in capitalist production and accounting the archetypal form of this rationalization ethos which, now stripped of its religious underpinnings, has profound implications for contemporary life.

Rationalization has three analytically separate but empirically intertwined elements: disenchantment, the result of the growth of science and secularization which undermines man's religiosity and the belief in ultimate spiritual and moral values; routinization, the inevitable consequence of an upsurge in creative charismatic leadership, involving the establishment of regular social routines, procedures and institutions; and bureaucratization. Weber sees the latter as becoming all-pervasive, given the growth of large-scale industry and government, which require efficient administrative structures if they are to run smoothly (Mommsen, 1974). Whilst admiring the rationality inherent in the logic of bureaucratization, he feared its consequences for human freedom and creativity. Whereas Marx had defined the problem of modern capitalist societies basically in terms of class exploitation, Weber sees it in the submission of man to huge oppressive bureaucracies which so structure his existence as to stifle his freedom and creative spirit. Bureaucratization is, moreover, one of the key problems in political life. He points to the lack of legislative control over the executive in

Germany, and compares it with the British situation where a different constitution and organized mass political parties provide some guarantee against the excesses of unchecked power. However, he recognizes that even political parties are undemocratic because bureaucratized, and hence are characterized by Michel's iron law of oligarchy. It is not, however, the lack of democracy or of egalitarianism which concerns him most. Weber was a pessimist, and an elitist, more concerned with Nietzschean questions regarding the conditions for adequate leadership, than with the issue of guaranteeing that political organization does not lead automatically to illegitimate political control.

In fact, Weber thought that the latter goal was an impossible one in modern societies. The issue of bureaucratization is central to Weber's analysis of socialism. Although he was in no position to engage in any sociological analysis of actual socialist revolutions (he died three years after the Russian Revolution), he argued that there was no fundamental discontinuity between capitalism and socialism, the latter being merely a logical extension of the former's rationalization tendencies. Even given common ownership of the means of production, the question of the 'means of administration' (Weber's term) remains. Socialism leads to nothing more than their appropriation by a new group who then become the new dominators (Weber, 1946b). Given his pessimistic view of human nature, it is hardly surprising that he argues that what appears on the surface to be a precondition for man's liberation leads in reality to little more than a further enslavement. Socialism means moreover the eradication of one of the few remaining embodiments of creativity: the independent entrepreneur.

It is unlikely, of course, that Weber was the originator of many of these ideas. He merely codified and articulated themes which were common in the first two decades of the twentieth century. Similar views on the inevitability of asymmetrical power relationships, their basis in natural human differences, the necessarily bureaucratized nature of any future socialist society and the lack of opportunities for human freedom are, of course, common ideological notions in much of contemporary social science as well as in common-sense consciousness, and had been prefigured in writers like de Tocqueville. It will be suggested later, in the chapter on ideology, that theoretical notions like those Weber was suggesting are tied in, in a complex way, with practical consciousness involved in the habits and routines which permeate everyday life.

Weber locates education within this framework. He wrote no books specifically on the topic and his sociology of education, whilst not unsystematic, has to be pieced together from his voluminous writings on such themes as stratification, bureaucratization, value freedom and the politicization of the universities. Whereas much of his general social theory has to be seen in the context of a dialogue with Marx, his writings on education have more to do with the legacy of Nietzsche (1909). (Weber wrote that any modern intellectual has to be appraised in the context of how he comes to terms with both thinkers.)

Implicit in Weber's work is a typology of education based upon his classification of different modes of domination and legitimation. This typology gives rise to two differing educational world views, the first oriented to the creation of the 'cultivated gentleman', the second to the moulding of professional expertise (Weber, 1946a and b). In the former, the educands are initiated into a holistic form of life of a status group, differentiated from the rest of society in terms of social prestige (Weber, 1946a). Such an education would not be narrowly utilitarian in scope but would involve an immersion into the magic and symbolism of a long-standing traditional culture. This is to be differentiated from an approach which trains the young in the specialized skills and knowledge demanded by specific occupational roles in the division of labour, and where bureaucratic structures are the main devourers of the educated. Weber suggests that the latter form tends to be narrower in range, leading to credentialism, as the educated have to demonstrate their particular competence to perform specific work-role requirements.

Weber's preference for the cultivated man over the expert (Weber, 1968) is self-evident in his various commentaries on contemporary changes in German universities (Weber, 1974). Like other nineteenth-century critics, Nietzsche and Stirner among others, he was critical of the way in which higher education was too closely geared to the training of personnel for the state, its civil and military bureaucracy, and of the lack of seriousness and application among students involved in their beer-drinking fraternities, for which Nietzsche had such contempt (Nietzsche, 1909). (It is alleged that Weber's own mother slapped his face when he returned one vacation from university whilst a student, exhausted and besotted with alcohol and high living (Weber, 1975).) However, above all, he is concerned about the encroachments on the liberal ideal of the independent scholar. This he sees as the result of two independent processes: the first deriving from increasing pressure from the state to appoint politically acceptable 'practical operators' over the heads of other, more distinguished scholars. The former,

Weber sees, 'will fit into academic machinery without further thought', to the detriment of the scholarly role of the university. Weber was accordingly greatly disturbed by what he saw as the personal injustice meted out to scholars like Sombart and Michels for their youthful involvement with Marxism, and by the discrimination experienced by Simmel who was a victim of anti-Semitism. The second source of threat to academe derived from what he described as the 'Americanization' of German universities, their transformation into 'capitalistic academic enterprises' organized along bureaucratic lines, controlled at their apex by Directors who were little more than 'academic entrepreneurs'. We may note here the favourable impression made by Veblen on Weber and the similarity in their position. Both lamented the demise of liberal scholarship, the precondition of which was independence. As Weber put it, the lack of economic independence is leading to a situation where the scholar's own means of production, his library, is being appropriated, and replaced by libraries financed and controlled by the state, with many dire consequences for intellectual freedom (Weber, 1974).

The main threat to the traditional role of the university, Weber suggests, is the politicization of the university where professors utilize their academic position to propagate their particular moral or political beliefs, thus allowing the impression that these are 'given' in 'the facts' rather than the result of arbitrary and irreducible moral choices. In a series of seminal papers which outline the liberal position on intellectual freedom, and the relationship between facts and values, he suggests that an academic's stance should be impartiality with respect to values, encouraging students to become more critically aware of the factual contingencies which are relevant to moral disputes so that they can make more responsible moral choices (Weber, 1949). Only through such value freedom in the face of the multiplicity of moral beliefs, all equally arbitrary, can the intellectual's personal integrity be safeguarded. Impartiality, however, should not be confused with ethical neutrality, which is the position many contemporary social scientists adopt, citing Weber in support.

The importance of Weber's idea of value freedom for contemporary thought about educational practice cannot be underestimated (Gouldner, 1973). It rests on the fetishized separation of education from politics which is an aspect of liberal theory, which will be commented upon at greater length in subsequent chapters. As was suggested earlier, the prescription that educators should avoid bias masks far more than it illuminates. In his own work, for example, there are all kinds of un-acknowledged and covert value preferences, the distorting effect of which Weber himself does not seem to recognize (Lewis, 1975).

Most of these biases relate to Weber's evaluation of capitalism: in particular his equation of capitalist rationality with rationality *per se*. Whereas Weber utilized an important distinction between formal and substantive rationality, arguing both their incompatibility and that there was thus 'some degree of irrationality in all economic systems' (Weber, 1964, p. 215) he believed that capitalist production in the hands of the individual entrepreneur and motivated by profit, embodied rationality. The limits of rationality in modern industrial societies were thus the limits of the capitalist system based upon formally free labour and commodity exchanges in the market place. For example, he thought that a planned economy where production decisions do not take place through the market mechanism would be inefficient, given the weakened incentive to labour (Weber, 1964, p. 214) and the lack of capitalist accounting. Apart from the bourgeois notion of man which he imports into his analysis of modern economic systems (Marcuse, 1968) he also finds it difficult to conceive of industrial societies as being anything other than highly bureaucratized. It is as if he is quite incapable of conceiving of any mode of organizing production outside of capitalist institutional forms. Capitalist industrialization becomes the necessary model of industrialization everywhere. He fails to see that the type of administrative bureaucracies which pertain under capitalism develop as a result of the imperative of profit-making, not of technology *per se*, from the need to stratify the labour force horizontally and vertically and generate a pyramidal command structure (Braverman, 1974). Indeed, it is in his conception of capitalist bureaucratization as a timeless universal necessity for solving problems of efficient organization, that his own deeply felt prejudices and political judgments are revealed. One can expect with some reason that the abolition of commodity production under socialism could lead to very different modes of organizing labour processes. Of particular significance would be the transcendence of the mental/manual division intrinsic to capitalist bureaucratization, which Weber seems to think necessarily follows from an efficiency requirement. As Marcuse has incisively argued, Weber's reason is in reality bourgeois reason. Bougeois reason is thus substantive unreason in that it does not lead to production for the satisfaction of human needs (Marcuse, 1968).

Weber does not consider the conflict between formal and substantive rationality under capitalism to be anything other than merely to do with the distribution of income. In any case, he argued that: 'If the standard used is that of the provision of a certain minimum of subsistence for the maximum size of the population the experiences of the last few decades would seem to show that formal and substantive rationality coincide to a relatively high degree' (Weber, 1964, p. 212). It should not need mentioning that the decades referred to saw the global expansion of European capitalism in imperialist annexations of the colonies, the great depression of the 1890s, heightened class conflict, and the events leading up to the First World War.

It is quite clear that Weber had no grasp of capitalism as a world system, no understanding of the crises and disequilibria built into the accumulation process and no appreciation of the substantive irrationality of the consequences of capitalist expansion into other parts of the world (Owen and Sutcliffe, 1972; Oxaal *et al.*, 1975). Perhaps he had been too influenced by the later work of Sombart, from whom he had largely learned his Marxism, who had argued that there was no evidence of the establishment of a world capitalist market; on the contrary, individual economies were becoming more self-sufficient (Luxemburg, 1951, p. 308).

Despite Weber's enormous erudition, and his fascination with the role of ideas in social life, it is clear that when it comes to a cool analytical appraisal of the ideology which sustains and legitimizes contemporary capitalism, he has little to offer. For example, whilst he has a series of perceptive insights about the conservative nature of the industrialized working class, he does not see these developments as tied in with the working out of the accumulation process on a world scale and the role of the state in maintaining hegemony. Neither does he discern how the changes within the university that he deplored might be related in some important way to the ongoing dynamic of the mode of production and its changing requirements at different conjunctures. Lacking a coherent theory of ideology which is appropriate to understand commodity fetishism, he fails to escape the ideological forms through which bourgeois society is apprehended.

It was suggested earlier that Weber was unashamedly bourgeois ('I do not deny my pride in this bourgeois descent' – Weber, 1974, p. 39). Perhaps more than any other social theorist, he has articulated in his sociology the necessary theoretical ideology which can serve as a reply to the counter-hegemonic critique of bourgeois society and bourgeois theory emanating from Marxism. However, although seeming to deal adequately with the phenomena of stratification and power, in reality he fails to penetrate to the heart of capitalism as a mode of production, a necessary precondition for making sense of the apparent complexity of stratification under capitalism. Later, the influence of Weberianism in contemporary sociology of education through Young, Bernstein, and Bourdieu will be considered. It is sufficient, at this stage, to conclude by positing that perhaps the key to Weber's ideological power in contemporary social thought lies in his discussion of value freedom. Weber's own life and work shows the political potential of an apparently impartial stance where intellectual work becomes seemingly detached from its practical roots. It seems that it is not only the 'practically useful scientific nonentities [in] academic posts' (1974, p. 44) who pose a threat to genuine understanding and scholarship but the broadly based erudition of a cultivated gentleman like Weber himself, whose ideology, making as science, performs an important class function, that of obscuring the class relations of domination and the way they are legitimated and sustained.

Weber's pessimism can be linked to the social and political events of his time and the vulnerability of a bourgeoisie that had never successfully achieved a bourgeois revolution and was threatened both from the left and the right. Durkheim shares none of that pessimism. On the contrary, whilst opposed to Marx's historical materialism, he at least believed in the possibility of utopia albeit somewhat different from that prefigured by Marx.

Emile Durkheim

If Comte is sometimes regarded as the founding father of modern sociology, Durkheim assuredly deserves his reputation as the sociologist of education, *par excellence*. Holding a joint chair in sociology and education at the University of Paris, he was the first to apply the new methods of sociology to develop a systematic conception of the nature and social functions of education and to articulate its practical implications for the state and society generally.

Like Veblen and Weber, we need to situate him in the specific social context from which emanated some of the central themes and preoccupations in his work. That context was France from the Franco-Prussian war to the First World War, an era during which, in the aftermath of the French Revolution, there had been a rapid development of industrialization accompanied by associated economic and social dislocations pervading all aspects of French society; and during which the weakness of the French state had been exposed in its collapse in the Franco-Prussian War, the fiasco of the short-lived Commune in 1870, the bloodshed and massacres which followed, and the class conflict and social unrest of the Third French Republic. Lukes has written of the sense of crisis which characterized intellectual life during this period (Lukes, 1973, p. 41). Three themes preoccupied Durkheim's generation: a strong patriotism, a sense of national decadence, and an urgent desire to contribute to the regeneration of France. All found their place in Durkheim's thinking.

Like that of his contemporaries, Veblen and Weber, Durkheim's work covers a prolific range of·substantive issues. It can be no part of this project to discuss them all. It suffices to single out four of the central themes in his writings in order to show how his analysis of the form and content of education was affected.

Durkheim's intellectual project can be regarded as an attempt to establish sociology as a legitimate field of enquiry, distinguished analytically from philosophy and ethics whilst by no means devoid of philosophical and moral content in its implications. In the journal which he and others founded in 1896, *Année Sociologique*, he attempted to combine the results of all the various social sciences into some more general, synthesizing framework which could provide the basis for more specialized work based upon an intellectual division of labour. Without in any way devaluing the role of specialized endeavour, Durkheim continually stressed the unity of the different social sciences and the need for a general conceptualization of society, its historical evolution and different manifestations through time, which could provide the basis for theoretical integration and coherence. Such a conceptualization depended upon a view of society as a reality *sui generis*, requiring a holistic methodology, irreducible to the study of individuals, and thus analytically prior to psychology which was merely the study of individual psyches.

Second, Durkheim was preoccupied with the changing basis of social solidarity, which, in his view, was inextricably intertwined with the social role of norms and values. Faced with a situation in which industrialization and secularization had disrupted the pre-industrial bases of social order in the family and the church, and where social dislocation and conflict were only too apparent, as revealed in the statistics of crime and suicide, or through the class conflicts which characterized the relationships between capital and labour, Durkheim's explanation of these social 'ills' was in terms of the lack of any intermediary social institutions between the family and the state which could overcome individualism and anomie and provide an effective basis for a reconstituted moral concensus and hence social stability. He was concerned to help generate a functional substitute for religion which could facilitate a higher mode of social integration based upon a more developed form of social solidarity resulting from specialization and mutual interdependence. Refusing to see social conflict as in any way following from inherent contradictions in the productive system, or the particular nature of the division of labour as resulting from the peculiar marriage of technological development and the needs of capitalist production for profit, he saw no intrinsic reason why modern complex societies could not be just as stable and integrated as their pre-industrial counterparts, albeit bound together by a more complex and differentiated value system (Durkheim, 1947).

In the third place, Durkheim sought to undermine the prevailing philosophical theory which purported to explain the relationship between the individual and society, the utilitarianism of Hobbes, Locke and Mill. Opposed to its basic assumption of human nature, that man was fundamentally asocial and motivated by individualistic, hedonistic desires, Durkheim developed the theory that human nature was only constituted within society, and that its particular character depended upon both the specific form of social organization which evolved in different historical contexts, and on the content of the 'collective representations' which were themselves socially generated. In Durkheim's view, society existed prior to the individual; it has to be seen as a moral order. Despite the plasticity of human nature, man only became so within and through participation in the social nexus. Even individuality itself is a social creation. Individual freedom, thus, has to be contained in some form of higher order so as not to undermine society and its moral authority. Human beings are in need of limits and moral discipline for it is only through submission to an authority which transcends the individual that man's rational and moral potential can be realized and his social nature grow to fruition.

Finally, in the idealist tradition of Kant and Descartes, Durkheim believed that through the new science of sociology there could be generated those practical insights and informed social policies which could improve social organization and advance social welfare in the direction of distributive justice and social harmony. Sociology could thus be the basis of a new secular ethic, which Durkheim thought so important to replace the role of religion in structuring social intercourse and defining the direction of social action. The analysis of what is, can thus contribute to the determination of what ought to be. Durkheim's educational theory has to be understood as an essential element of these moral and political concerns. His analysis of education is developed in what were essentially lectures delivered to students destined for careers in the educational system. Given his faith in the potential of sociology for developing a new secular morality and in the light of his explanation of social unrest in terms of the lack of moral integration, it is hardly surprising that he should place such great emphasis on the key significance of education for generating social cohesion. For Durkheim, education is related to sociology as practice is to theory (Lukes, 1973). It involves the realization within society of the practical insights which emanate from social analysis.

In line with Durkheim's rejection of any essentialist concept of human nature, he repudiates the possibility of developing a theory of education which is universally applicable, arguing against the thesis that 'there is one ideal and perfect education which applies to all men indiscriminately'. He similarly opposes any prescriptive definition in terms of its role in enhancing individual well-being, happiness or perfection. Instead, he advocates a non-evaluative definition of what education, considered sociologically, comprises: the influence exercised by adults deliberately upon the young. In so defining it, he recognizes its historical variability through time, and in different kinds of societies, and the fact that it is only in certain types of societies that specialized educational institutions develop, or that a specialized social category of educated people becomes sociologically significant (Durkheim, 1961b; 1956; 1976).

For Durkheim, therefore, it is society that defines the structure and content of education: 'the man education should realize in us is not man as nature made him, but man as society wishes him to be, and it wishes him to be such as its internal economy dictates' (Durkheim, 1956, p. 122). He sees the social function of education, accordingly, as the transmission of the particular set of shared moral and cognitive beliefs on which the survival of a particular form of social organization depends. The values, language, norms, and cognitions, which form the stuff of that which is transmitted through education, thus vary from society to society, given the way they are inextricably entwined with the differentiated structures of societies. It would, therefore, be both foolish and undesirable to prescribe a particular content for education which would be valid for all time. Moreover, not only is there no education which is universally valid for the whole species, but there is no society in which different pedagogical systems do not coexist and function side by side, given the existence of different castes, classes and localities, and the requirements of occupational specialization. Thus, in addition to stressing education's role in transmitting common values and cognitions, Durkheim also recognizes its role in providing for specialization of function, in the teaching of the specific skills, attitudes and norms which role differentiation requires.

When considering education's role in social allocation, Durkheim argues that the specific roles which people occupy are not determined by nature or by intellectual and moral temperament: if we specialize, it is not for reasons which lie uniquely within us. It is society that determines the form that specialization takes (Durkheim, 1956). Durkheim concedes that specialization means that we do not develop all our abilities and potential to their fullest degree. To the extent that we cultivate some attributes, others atrophy. We give up a part of ourselves in order to realize our essential sociality. However, he does not see this as a problem, since we can only become human in and through society, and all societies are internally differentiated in terms of their role-structure, however simple the form of their social organization.

Despite the level of complexity and the degree of specialization within society, a function of the extent of the division of labour, Durkheim emphasizes that education has a social function to play in initiating the young into those over-arching moral values which bind societies together. Whilst the content of these may vary, as we have seen, there are certain components of moral systems which are universal. All encourage within us the spirit of self-discipline and self-control, a sense of self-abnegation and positive attachment to the group to which we belong, and the spirit of autonomy. Despite variation, therefore, in the moral basis of social solidarity, its rationale is always the same, the fostering of the necessary preconditions for society's survival and hence of the well-being of its inhabitants.

We should not over-emphasize the moral functions of education to the detriment of its cognitive components. Durkheim's views on this issue are well developed in *The Evolution of Educational Thought* (Durkheim, 1976). However, in addition to this work, he also developed a sociology of knowledge in *The Elementary Forms of the Religious Life* (1961) and in *Primitive Classification* (with Marcel Mauss) (1963), in which he tried to identify empirically the social roots of the fundamental categories of cognition. Whilst he did not directly apply these ideas to the cognitive dimension of educational knowledge, their potential should be obvious. The insight that symbolic categories for ordering experiences are sociologically contingent, and that they may be linked in some way with forms of social organization and structure, has proved extraordinarily fruitful even though there are many difficulties with the details of Durkheim's formulation (Lukes, 1973). This hypothesis did not, however, lead him to a position of epistemological relativism as in some recent strands in the sociology of education, as will be discussed below. In his view, whilst the content of mind might vary, the criteria of truth and rationality are universal. He was quintessentially a representative of the French rationalist tradition, believing in the power of reason which transcends any particular cosmology. He therefore rejected both moral and epistemological relativism. The task of education is thus to propagate those common moral and intellectual beliefs which society in its evolution has proved to be historically necessary, and hence objective, and so to prepare people for their social role.

Having outlined the elements of Durkheim's theory, the fundamental question remains the extent to which his approach provides a superior conceptualization of the social functions of education to that of Weber and Veblen. Without denying the validity and brilliant originality of some of his ideas, in particular the stress on the social genesis of what it means to be educated and hence the historical variability of educational contents, the conclusion has to be that, certainly for class societies, his model has serious deficiencies. The fundamental weaknesses all stem from a central problem, his conceptualization of society and his analysis of the basis of social order in terms of common value systems. These deficiencies will be considered in the context of his discussion of industrial societies, although the issues raised have more general relevance to the whole of Durkheim's work.

We have seen how one of his overriding preoccupations concerns the changing basis of social solidarity with the advance in the division of labour which accelerates with industrialization. He saw no reason to predict a necessary diminution of social solidarity, only a change in the content of the collective representations compared with that which obtains under mechanical solidarity. However, in *The Division of Labour in Society* (1947), he made a distinction between its normal forms and abnormal manifestations, the former leading to social order,

31

the latter to conflict and other symptoms of social pathology. He describes three kinds of abnormal forms: anomic, non-interdependent, and forced. From Durkheim's elaboration of these it is quite clear that what he defines as *abnormal* may, in reality, be unavoidable and hence normal under capitalism (Gouldner, 1959). For example, one criterion he offers for abnormality is when individuals are forced to occupy social roles which are incommensurate with their talents, i.e. when equality of opportunity is lacking: 'Labour is only divided spontaneously when society is divided in such a way that social inequalities express natural inequalities' (quoted in Lukes, 1973). Despite the problem with his concept of 'natural inequalities', given that he had himself emphasized the social determinants of socialization, even if there are such inequalities, equality of opportunity nowhere exists in a capitalist society because structured inequality in the social division of labour tends to reproduce itself, through the labour process, the educational system and through the political arena. Individuals are consequently normally 'forced' to occupy social roles incommensurate with their 'talents'. He also suggests that an abnormal form exists where contracts within the market are unjust: where 'the price of the object bears no relationship to the labour it costs or the service it renders' (1947, p. 376). Durkheim seems to believe that 'reciprocity in equivalence of exchange or services' is possible within a market society. He ignores the fact that behind the backs of the direct producers (Marx, 1974), given the appropriation of the means of production by capitalists in the form of private property, which produces thereby a wage-labour force who have no ownership of productive resources beyond their own labour-power, there exists structured inequality which renders the idea of a just contract somewhat bizarre and mystifying. It also renders the third criterion which Durkheim proposed for abnormality problematic: the enforced maintenance of social order, presumably to compensate for the breakdown or failure of normative constraint, which is what obtains when the division of labour is functioning normally. It can be contended that had Durkheim followed Marx's analysis of the internal dynamics of the capitalist mode of production (Gouldner, 1959) and had he operated with some concept of ideology, he would have realized the oversimplifications built into the notion of normative regulation. In class societies generally, and in capitalist societies specifically, where there is private property in the means of production, and where the profit motive provides the main dynamism, the preconditions for the normal forms of the division of labour cannot obtain, and hence education cannot be other than a system for reproducing capitalist production relationships, and the ideological forms of social consciousness which help to legitimate and maintain them.

Durkheim's blindness emanates from two interrelated assumptions which are characteristic of much bourgeois social theory. On the one hand he adheres to a structural-functionalist theory of stratification, seeing it as functional, necessary and inevitable, related to 'natural' variations in talents and the differential functional importance of the various social roles; on the other, he fails to discern how capitalism generates a specific form of the division of labour, characterized by structured inequality, in part deliberately fostered and in part structurally maintained. Thus when he postulates no inherent conflict between specialization and moral unity, he has not recognized that specialization itself may be associated with different kinds of social rewards in terms of power, economic opportunities or status, and that such stratification must inevitably generate conflict and different and possibly competing class cultures. His only way out would be to postulate that the content of society's collective representations would itself provide the legitimations and rationales both for inequality as such and for each individual's location within such a structure of inequality. It is precisely in relation to this issue that a concept of ideology would be helpful, but Durkheim fails to develop such a notion. This is because he conceives of a consensually based social order: there is no inherent contradiction between the interests of society as a whole and particular groups within it. As a result he does not explore the ideological potential of so-called shared collective representations for furthering and legitimating the interests of classes in power. Whilst he cannot but be aware of the existence of different classes, he believes that there is no inherent antagonism between them. For example, in his debate with Lagardelle (the revolutionary syndicalist) over the issue of patriotism and class conflict, he clearly advocates a policy of class collaboration, offering the justification that every class is part of a larger social whole which potentially guarantees the interests of all classes. After all, they 'inhale the same moral atmosphere, they are, though they deny it, members of a single society, and as a result cannot but be impregnated with the same ideas' (Durkheim, quoted in Lukes, 1973). Those who utilize a concept of ideology would not disagree with the sentiments expressed. However, they would profoundly oppose the implications that Durkheim draws from such a notion, that the organization of society serves the interests of all

33

classes, or that the wide acceptance of such ideas develops spontaneously.

Durkheim was unsympathetic to any form of class analysis of capitalist society. He rejected the materialist conception of history and the hypothesis of the centrality of production and economic factors in historical change. He almost directly inverted the Marxian thesis of substratum and suprastructure. In Durkheim's theory the substratum was religion. 'All other manifestations of collective activity, including law, art, political and economic forms are secondary and derivative. They are not, however, merely passive; the economic, for example, can partially modify the very substratum from which it results' (Durkheim, 1897, quoted in Lukes), but even the single most dynamic factor in social change in contemporary society, science, has its origins in religion and moral representations: 'the fundamental notions of science are of a religious origin' (Durkheim, 1961, p. 616).

Directly opposed to any materialist view of historical change, Durkheim articulates an idealist view of society and history. The state, for example, is regarded as the rational conscious centre, a benign institution above society, a moral force which is capable of directing social organization in the interests of social harmony and economic regulation. He does not define it as a Marxist would, as an aspect of class domination embodying systematic structural biases which work for the furtherance of powerful interests. Nor does he see the state in Weberian terms, as the instrument which monopolizes legitimate force. For Durkheim, the state is an essentially moral phenomenon.

In the years prior to the First World War, Durkheim was associated quite closely with the Solidarists, a group who might be seen as the French counterpart of the Fabian Society. Opposed to the extremes of class inequality, and rejecting the resurgence of Marxist interpretations of capitalism, they supported the 'idea of justice as a repayment of a social debt by the privileged to the underprivileged, assuming mutual interdependent and quasi contractual obligations between all citizens and implying a programme of public education, social insurance, labour and welfare legislation' (Hayward, 1959). Along with the Solidarists, Durkheim advocated the extension of state economic planning, its enlarged welfare function and a middle way between *laissez-faire* capitalism and collectivism based upon a commitment to distributive justice (Lukes, 1973, p. 350). He did not, however, share their belief in the moral necessity of private property, or their faith in legislative reformism without a prior moral regeneration. The latter required, in his view, a social basis in new institutional forms within which such problems as the inequitable distribution of income could be resolved.

It was in this context that he proposed the setting up of occupational associations which could take over some of the moral functions no longer performed by the family or the church, in order to 'moralize economic life' and provide some solutions to the problem of anomie engendered by unrestrained individualistic materialism (Durkheim, 1957).

It is not that Durkheim was blind to the ills of capitalism but that his explanations were framed primarily in moral and cultural terms, as were his solutions. He saw no future in any political strategy premised on class antagonism. The risk was too high in that there might be an undermining of authority, which could not, in his view, be regenerated spontaneously. He believed that social harmony and progress could be achieved by social policies based upon science and reason, with education providing the appropriate climate and enlightened leadership. The similarity between Durkheim and the later Mannheim is only too apparent. The moral pathologies of capitalist societies are not inherent, merely abnormal. They dictate moral solutions.

Unlike Weber, Durkheim was an optimist. In the tradition of French rationalism, he never succumbed to that loss of self-confidence, the retreat into nihilism and irrationalism which pervaded much bourgeois intellectual life in his period (Hughes, 1959). He will now be compared with Mannheim, who, although writing somewhat later, embodies some crucial continuities with Durkheim.

Karl Mannheim

In discussing the work of Mannheim alongside that of Veblen, Weber and Durkheim, it is not intended to give the impression that his intellectual stature is comparable or his contribution to social history as seminal. The reasons for considering him are threefold. First, his early work on the social bases of knowledge and its implication for problems of epistemology and truth, has often been cited as of some importance for a sociology of education which wishes to focus on knowledge or the curriculum. Second, since his early work was centrally preoccupied with the kinds of issues that concerned Marx and Weber, whereas his later work was in a more policy-oriented, Fabian reformist tradition, he can be regarded as something of a link figure between the classical founders of the discipline and its contemporary exponents. Finally, it was Mannheim who, with regard to the sociology of education in Britain in particular, played a significant role in influencing its direction in the first two decades after the Second World War. It is therefore of some interest to examine the context within which his thought and its inherent limitations evolved.

Mannheim's thought underwent a number of important changes. To some extent this may have been due to his being forced to change his country of residence several times as the political events of the inter-war years in central Europe caught up with him. He was born in Budapest into a middle-class Jewish family of Hungarian and German parents. Whilst at the university of Budapest he formed part of a group of left-wing intellectuals which included Lukàcs and a number of other well-known writers and thinkers of that period (Remmling, 1975). However, in 1920 Mannheim was forced to emigrate to Germany after the crushing of a short-lived socialist revolution which he had supported and to some extent participated in. There, he held a number of university posts, ending up at Frankfurt where he became Professor of sociology and political economy. In 1933, with the rise of Hitler, Mannheim was dismissed from his post and went to England, where, befriended by people like Lord Beveridge, Maurice Ginsberg and Harold Laski, he found a home at the London School of Economics. In 1945 he accepted a chair in education at the University of London and began to teach sociology and education.

Most of his earliest work concerned questions of epistemology conducted from within an idealist framework, but not long after his move to Germany he began to investigate more fully the social context of intellectual systems. This may have been the result of his exposure to the lively controversies still raging in Germany about the methodology of the social sciences which led him to begin to ponder on the substantive relevance of the social sciences to issues which he had previously considered almost entirely within the framework of philosophy. It was during this period that he became more familiar with and receptive to the thought of Marx, partly as a result of his interest in the work of Lukàcs, and also of Weber, with whom he shared a house at one time.

He began to think systematically about the various existential influences on the form and content of ideas. Ideas, he asserted, are not the mere products of creative minds, thinking in a vacuum, but develop within a socially generated style of thinking which has a 'functional dependence . . . on the differentiated social reality standing behind it' (Mannheim, 1960, p. 190). In a brilliant essay on conservative thought, for example (Mannheim, 1952), he compared the structure and themes of conservative thinking in Germany in the first half of the nineteenth century with that of liberal and proletarian thought. Drawing similarities and contrasts with France and England, he shows how the peculiarities of German conservatism have to be related to the specificities of a declining feudal class in a context where the bourgeoisie has never attained a dominant political position or an independent autonomous ideology. There are in this essay many suggestive insights which could be utilized in a study of the content of educational knowledge, for example, or of the history of educational theory in different social formations.

During his stay in Germany, Mannheim wrote extensively on the way in which such social factors as class, occupational group, generation, the ethos of competition and so on, impinged upon social thinking. His best-known work was *Ideology and Utopia* (1960), which pursued, in particular, the theme of the relationship between class position and world outlook. Drawing on Marx, Weber and Dilthey, Mannheim developed a two-fold classification of ideological systems; those he called ideologies, which were characteristic of backward-looking classes having a vested interest in the maintenance of the *status quo*, and Utopias, which were generated by subordinate classes who had an interest in transcending the present state of social organization in order to substitute something better. Whilst recognizing that utopian thought was an important impetus to social change and dynamism, Mannheim denied the status of objective truth to either. Both merely reflected a partial perspective, a one-sided viewpoint.

Mannheim's work came under criticism from the right and the left. From the right it was accused of being nihilistic, relativistic, anti-idealist and a danger to the unifying belief in 'Germany and the German mission' (Curtius, 1932, quoted in Remmling, 1975). He replied to a number of these charges in 'Problems of Sociology in Germany' (in Wolff, 1971). From the left, however, he was accused of using Marx's concept of ideology against Marxism itself, transforming dialectical concepts into static classificatory schemas. Representatives of the Frankfurt School were especially critical. Mannheim had, they thought, distorted Marx's notion of the dialectic. He had substituted for a notion of contradiction at the structural level of political economy, a purely idealist conception of groups in struggle over competing ideas and world views. 'It calls everything into question and criticises nothing'

(Adorno, 1967). Moreover, whereas Marx was concerned with theory *and* praxis, Mannheim's work was seen as little more than the abstract contemplations of a bourgeois social scientist. Nothing seemed to follow politically from his analysis.

But for Mannheim, something did follow. It was during this time that he began to develop the notion (derived from Alfred Weber) of a socially free floating intelligentsia, who, uncontaminated by the practical interests which motivate classes, could somehow penetrate below the ideological content of thought, and achieve, at least to some extent, a more objective synthesis. It is to these groups that Mannheim would turn in his later work as the key to the implementation of his ideas on social planning and the democratic state (1940, 1951b).

Mannheim never gave a satisfactory account as to why he thought intellectuals were somehow immune from bias and detached from social class and other influences. As we have seen in our discussion of Weber, Veblen and Durkheim, intellectuals are just as likely to perpetrate ideology as any other social group. Mannheim seemed to think that their objectivity derives from their education, but of course, the content of education itself is infused with ideology and not somehow immune from social interest. One wonders what Mannheim himself thought of the widespread capitulation of German academics in the face of national socialism. Even he, however, seemed unaware of precisely what threat was presented by Hitler and his Nazi party. He could still, in the early 1930s, be relatively optimistic about the future of Weimar Germany and the role that intellectuals could, and should, play in its future direction (Remmling, 1975).

Despite his experience of Nazi Germany and the horrors of the Second World War, Mannheim never relinquished his faith in intellectuals, even though they had been prevented, in his view, from carrying out their historic role by the pressure emanating from mass society. It is through a consideration of the latter that he arrived at his explanation of fascism and other forms of totalitarianism such as communism (in Mannheim's assessment) (Mannheim, 1943). He suggested that twentieth-century democratization had led to a degeneration of traditional cultural elites because the criteria of achievement had given way to an obsession with equalizing opportunity. This had led to a situation where the culturally and politically unsophisticated masses had succeeded in infiltrating leadership groups, resulting in a 'leadership of the essentially unqualified' (quoted in Floud, 1969) and a loss of self-confidence among the intelligentsia. As a result, the forces of irrationalism prevailed and sober rational leadership was eschewed in favour of an appeal to impulse and emotion. Mannheim was no egalitarian in his later life. He was a supporter of the idea of *Standesgesellschaft*, a hierarchical society in which intellectuals are offered a special position by virtue of the superiority of their culture and insights. This did not mean a return to liberal *laissez-faire* capitalism with its potential for social conflict, but an inauguration of a carefully planned society in which the intelligentsia could play its role of enlightened leadership. It is not difficult to see the effect which his stay in England was having on him. Mannheim regarded England as a model of a stable democratic society in which intellectuals combined with politicians to advise on those policies best suited for slow evolutionary but planned social change through compromise and the application of reason. The London School of Economics, for example, where Mannheim taught for a time, was the intellectual hothouse for those social reformist policies like the Beveridge Plan which promised to inaugurate a new future, uncontaminated by class conflict, after the end of the Second World War.

In association with a group of rather conservative Christian humanists, including T.S. Eliot and John Middleton Murry, organized in an association called the Moot, Mannheim developed a strategy based upon the dual institutions of religion and education. Both could foster the appropriate values for a consensual social order, a sense of direction and purpose, and diffuse a receptive attitude towards planned social change. In the latter part of his life, he was mainly concerned with questions of leadership. (T.S. Eliot acknowledges his debt to Mannheim in *Notes Towards a Definition of Culture* (1963) in which he advanced the view that culture could only ever be enjoyed by a minority.) However, Mannheim thought it important to develop and expand the education of the masses since it was in them that the potential for irrationality and social disorder primarily lay. Attempting to define a 'third way' between 'the *laissez faire* principle and the new principle of regulation', his views amount to little more than a commitment to a mixed economy in which an enlightened welfare state, guided by rational, well-educated advisers, carries out those social policies which are efficient, avoid the extremes of poverty and the anarchy of the market, and are conducive to social cohesion. He did not think it necessary to advocate the abolition of private property. Indeed, he regarded private entrepreneurial business as an excellent training ground for leadership and as a protection against a surfeit of bureaucratization. The resemblances to Weber are striking.

His views on education are essentially prescriptive rather than analytical. He wanted to broaden the concept of education to include all those institutions capable of effecting some educative influence not only on the young but also on adults (Mannheim and Stewart, 1962). The masses should be the object of an enlightened social policy designed to create the appropriate framework of values within which social life could be orderly conducted. He advocated such policies as re-education, lifelong education, relevant education, education for leisure, an end to over-specialization and the introduction of group pedagogical techniques. In short, he expounded educational policies which have since become an integral part of the enlightened liberal educator's vocabulary.

Jean Floud has described Mannheim as a 'utopian of the right seeking the security of an integrated society grounded in a common morality inculcated through education'. She draws comparisons with Durkheim, suggesting that despite their different scholarly pedigrees and styles, they were both 'haunted by a sense of social disorder and crisis and made it their life work to seek a solution to the intractable problems of consensus in modern society' (Floud, 1969). Despite the similarities, however, Mannheim in England never seemed to regain the intellectual creativity of the earlier period. In 1931 and 1934, for example, he wrote some incisive commentaries on the comparative strengths and weaknesses of German and American sociology which reveal that at that time he held to some rigorous criteria regarding what constitutes an adequate sociology, criteria by which his own subsequent work may be found sadly wanting (Mannheim, 1953). Had his 'studies on questions of practical detail . . . [remained] alive to the great theoretical problems which pervade and co-ordinate with each other all the scattered empirical facts' (Mannheim, 1953, p. 194), he might have been less obsessed with prescriptive social policies and more concerned to elucidate the underlying causes of the symptoms of social disorder he wished to eradicate. Despite the promise of his earlier work and the social and political importance of the questions he set himself to resolve – why fascism? how to plan for a rational society in which freedom and liberty reigned? – he never developed an adequate holistic theoretical framework with which to generate answers. He lacked any conception of the dynamics of monopoly capitalism, the workings of political economy and the connections between these and political processes as did the other thinkers discussed above. Such defects in his perspective are only too apparent in his analysis of fascism or of the welfare state. He does not see the necessity of pursuing a class analysis of the state, whether fascist or social democratic. Nor does he operate with a theoretical concept of capitalism as a mode of production. In line with the dominant strand in liberal social theory, his diagnoses of social problems are primarily phrased in cultural terms, as also are his solutions – the resort to education and religion. He fails to escape the tyranny of liberal common sense, even in his discussion of the medium whereby religious and educational solutions are to be affected, namely via a benevolent leadership of the intelligentsia.

As soon as one begins to question Mannheim's notion of a socially unattached intelligentsia, the defects in his ideal of planning become apparent. In liberal theory, the continuation of many social problems is often explained by the lack of adequate knowledge, or alternatively, of funds to operationalize available knowledge. In contrast, in Marxist theory the key obstacle is often found to be the existing class relationships with their asymmetrical power, which often prevents what needs to be done from being done. Mannheim's later work lacks a sociological concept of power. Consequently, the political difficulties of his concept of planning are only too evident. As Adorno warned:

> Mannheim's reflections, nourished by liberal commonsense, all amount to the same thing in the end – recommending social planning without ever penetrating to the foundations of society. . . . The answer is to be found not in the reactionary postulate of its 'rootedness in Being' but rather in the reminder that the very intelligentsia that pretends to float freely is fundamentally rooted in the very being that needs to be changed and which it merely pretends to criticize. For it, the rational is the optimal functioning of the system, which postpones the catastrophe without asking whether the system in its totality is not in fact the optimum in irrationality. (Adorno, 1967, p. 48).

It would be a worthwhile exercise to apply some of Mannheim's insights in his earlier work on the sociology of knowledge to his own writings on social planning. Using his hypothesis of the class origin and functions of different systems of thought, one might suggest that his essentially gradualist and reformist approach to social improvement, his commitment to the welfare state and social planning, are characteristic of a bourgeois class attempting, through a strategy of class of collaboration, to resolve a potential crisis in social hegemony engendered by the excesses of the market place. Despite his earlier preference for utopian thought as opposed to ideology, Mannheim's whole perspective can only be regarded as fundamentally reactionary in that he fails to develop any fundamental analysis of the dynamics of capitalist relations of production and their consequences, which at one level he is trying to reform.

It is precisely in this respect that there is a fundamental continuity between his work and that of his successors in the next two decades in the sociology of education. Self-consciously prescriptive, and an unashamed believer in the potential of the welfare state to reform and liberalize capitalism, he at least makes no pretence of conflating the notion of scientific objectivity with ethical and ideological neutrality (Remmling, 1975, p. 109). Sociologists are exhorted to engage in the task of defining the direction of social reconstruction (Mannheim, 1943), a prescription which set the pattern for the 1950s and early 1960s, when the problem of equality of opportunity became the main theme of the discipline. This theme is still a recurring one in the work of the authors to be discussed in Chapter 3.

Conclusion

Although this critique has attempted to point out the deficiencies of these theorists' understanding of the dynamics of capitalism, suggesting that in their various ways they are all, to some extent, prisoners of the basic assumptions of bourgeois thought, it is no part of the argument that they do not deserve careful study. The sheer range of their thought, their eschewal of any narrow specialization, their moral and political impetus, their commitment to theory and rejection of mindless empiricism, fully warrant their place in the history of the sociology of education. Indeed, in comparison with much that passes for the sociology of education in the present day, their insights are of far greater significance for the liberal position. They represent some of the high points in bourgeois social theorizing about education. Nevertheless, it is as exponents of a theoretical ideology that they have been examined, an ideology that, to a lesser or greater extent, fails to transcend the limits of bourgeois society. It is now appropriate to consider three contemporary theorists to ascertain whether their work provides a more adequate framework for understanding education in capitalist societies.

3 The sociology of the curriculum: a critique

In Chapter 1 the specialization process within knowledge was seen to affect the development of the sociology of education, producing a fragmentation into a number of discrete fields of enquiry. The emergent sociology of the curriculum is one such field which has, during the last decade, established itself institutionally through specialized courses, textbooks (Eggleston, 1977; Young, 1971b; Musgrave, 1973) and research priorities. In this chapter, rather than attempting a comprehensive overview of all that passes for the sociology of the curriculum, the work of three theorists will be examined. Bernstein, Bourdieu and Young have been singled out because, more than any others, they have provided some theoretical guidelines for the study of the content of the curriculum. However, the theme here will be that despite the importance of some of their insights, considered in isolation, a significant break with some key assumptions of bourgeois social theory concerning the nature of capitalism and of education is required. None of them has successfully managed to achieve that theoretical rupture although Michael Young is evolving in that direction. The implications of such a move will be elaborated upon more fully in Chapters 4 and 5.

Before commencing the analysis, two important questions must be raised. The first concerns the scope of a sociology of the curriculum. Bernstein suggests a broad focus. In a now famous quotation he suggests that 'How a society selects, classifies, distributes, transmits and evaluates the educational knowledge it considers to be public, reflects both the distribution of power and the principles of social control' (Bernstein, 1971a). He views such issues as part of a broader focus: the structure of cultural transmission. The central question thus becomes the relationship between power and control on the one hand, and the content of education on the other.

In Marxist theory, the key power relationships in society are those of class, which have simultaneously economic, political and ideological dimensions. If we accept Bernstein's concerns, a theory of the curriculum must be embedded in a theory of class, and the mechanisms of class reproduction.

The second and related question concerns the possibility of developing a general theory of cultural reproduction which is not simultaneously profoundly historical and empirical. Since capitalist production takes place within specific historical conditions which vary in relationship to different problems of capital accumulation, the course of class struggles and alliances in each national context, a *general* theory of the curriculum risks being overly formalistic. Without a holistic and historical methodology capable of penetrating the specificities of capitalist development in varying conditions, the analysis of the curriculum must degenerate into a series of oversimplifications and platitudes. Our analysis must thus be a history as broad as that of capitalist class society itself. It is in the light of these considerations that the analysis of Bernstein, Bourdieu and Young proceeds.

Basil Bernstein

In a recent commentary on his own work, Bernstein (1975) elaborated what he regards as the necessary elements of a theory of cultural reproduction or transmission. Its central focus would be the 'matrix of transmission': the structures and processes by which the principles which underlie social order are transmitted and realized through various institutional forms such as the family, education, work and leisure. The transmission process has both macro and micro dimensions. It is affected by the class structure, the polity, the division of labour and the dominant cultural principles or codes through which social order is regulated. It also realizes through linguistic and other social codes in specific social contexts the mental structures of our consciousness. Bernstein represented this theoretical framework diagrammatically in the Introduction to *Class Codes and Control*, vol. 3 (Bernstein, 1975).

Bernstein's papers on educational transmission, especially 'On the classification and framing of educational knowledge' (1971) and 'Class and Pedagogies: Visible and Invisible' (in Bernstein, 1975), have been regarded as of critical significance for those seeking to develop a sociology of education which defines the management of knowledge as the focal concern. These papers are full of stimulating insights which only the most churlish anti-Durkheimian would wish to ignore. It is not intended to carry out a detailed textual appraisal of these two papers. The issue is rather whether Bernstein's work provides a starting point

44

for an adequate analysis of the relationship between ideology, knowledge and schooling. In this section it will be argued that, whatever the obvious brilliance of many of the observations, the theoretical underpinnings of his work have many shortcomings and are inadequate as a basis for a fruitful synthesis. It is suggested that an alternative problematic, emanating from the Marxist tradition, is more appropriate.

Bernstein cites both Durkheim and Marx as his leading sociological mentors. He has expressed his debt to Durkheim in the following way: 'I have yet to find any social theorist whose ideas are such a source, at least to me, of understanding of what the term *social* entails' (1975, p. 17). Similarly, 'Durkheim's work is a truly magnificent insight into the relationships between symbolic orders, social relationships and the structuring of experience' (1973, p. 194). Concerning Marx, he has written:

> Although Marx is less concerned with the internal structure and process of transmission of symbolic systems, he does give us a key to their institutionalization and change. The key is given in terms of the social significance of society's productive system and the power relationships to which the productive system gives rise. Further, access to, control over, . . . and change in critical symbolic systems, according to the theory, is governed by power relationships as these are embodied in the class structure. It is not only capital in the strict economic sense which is subject to appropriation, manipulation and exploitation but also cultural capital in the form of the symbolic systems through which man can extend and change the boundaries of his experience. (1975, p. 196).

Bernstein summarizes his theoretical indebtedness in the following way: 'Essentially I have used Durkheim and Marx at the macro level and Mead at the micro level' (1973, p. 196).

Karabel and Halsey (1977, p. 71), in a recent overview of the sociology of education, have suggested that, whilst Bernstein is a self-confessed Durkheimian, his recent work, especially the two papers mentioned above, illustrate a movement beyond a mere convergence between Durkheimianism and Marxism in the direction of a new synthesis. They emphasize the timely nature of such a synthesis 'between his own work which draws widely upon both the interpretative and functionalist schools, and the research of the Marxist and Weberian conflict theorists. . . . The possibilities of theoretical and empirical advance through a synthesis of Marxist and Weberian and Bernsteinian views of social and educational change are manifold' (p. 71).

We do not wish to speculate on whether a synthesis of a range of approaches resting on very different epistemological and theoretical assumptions is either possible or desirable. Bernstein himself makes a similar point in another context. It is more important to consider the proposition made by Karabel and Halsey, in the context of a discussion of Bernstein's relationship with Marxism:

> In recent years, . . . Bernstein has shown signs of moving towards a thorough going confrontation with Marxism, and such an effort, which would entail an attempt to integrate his theory of education and cultural transmission with the Marxist analysis of the place of the educational system in the larger social structure would be a highly productive enterprise. (70)

An alternative view of Berstein which will be argued here is that, despite his use of Marxist categories, he has never engaged in a confrontation with Marxism, that his problematic remains firmly within the terrain of bourgeois social science, that his theoretical framework is incapable of entering into a creative synthesis with Marxism and that the latter problematic is vastly superior to resolve the kinds of issues with which his work is concerned. Moreover, we shall suggest that his increasing resort to Marxist terms tells us more about the intellectual context in which Bernstein is now writing, and his potential audience, rather than reflecting any significant movement of his theoretical framework away from its structural-functionalist beginnings.

This is not the place to provide a comprehensive overview of Bernstein's work. We shall comment subsequently on his contribution to the understanding of the role of language in the reproduction of class relationships. Instead, we wish to isolate several themes in his work which are relevant to a consideration of the relationship between the problem of ideology and the social role of schooling, and discuss his relationship to Marxism in that context.

Bernstein's method

Bernstein has described his method as one which moves from the micro to the macro levels of analysis (1975, p. 2). This is not because he is unaware of the wider context within which interactions occur but because of his confessed difficulty in moving to the macro analysis,

> until I had some grip upon the local relationships at the micro aspect. . . . I think it is possibly because I am sensitive to interactions and once these are part of my experience, I can begin to

intuit what I take to be the structural principles which they embody. (1975, p. 2)

In short, through moving from the micro to the macro he has 'tried to develop a way of thinking which integrates structural and interactional categories so that a theory of transmission might be possible' (1975, p. 32). In the same article, he also maintains that he does not find 'the customary distinction between macro and micro (two levels) helpful' (1975, p. 20). Whilst one may agree with him on the latter point, it is clear that Bernstein's 'intuitions' of structural categories derive from a notion of society as a descriptive pre-given rather than as a theoretically constructed object (Stedman Jones, 1976). When, for example, he discusses the micro contexts of the family or the school, embedded in his analysis is an implicit model of the macro structure apprehended ideologically within the terms of bourgeois sociology. For example, he makes frequent reference to 'our pluralistic society' with its differentiated value systems and its trend towards individualistic, personally differentiated role orientations, compared with 'monolithic societies' which have single value systems and in which the educational system is a major instrument of political socialization. One is provided with no criteria to distinguish pluralistic from monolithic societies beyond the surface considerations of value systems, nor any basis for deciding when educational systems do *not* perform a crucial role in political legitimation. Moreover, whilst he frequently cites the economic system, the class structure, the division of labour, power relations and dominant and dominating value systems as important constraining elements upon any micro interaction, he provides us with no theoretical concepts for their analysis or for apprehending their interrelationships. We will elaborate further on this issue when discussing Bernstein's description and analysis of contemporary social changes, and the class structure. Meanwhile it is necessary to reiterate how very differently a Marxist would conceptualize the macro context within which interactions take place.

The basic conceptual category of historical materialism is that of mode of production. History is periodized in terms of distinctions between different modes of production and their complex articulation in different situations. Rather than using the term society Marxists use the concept of social formation. The latter refers to a historically specific combination of different modes of production in articulation with each other, of which one is usually dominant. Each social formation has its own unique specificity, given its peculiar historical genesis, but shares features in common with others in which the same mode of production is dominant. Marxism does not differentiate societies in terms of such factors as the degree of value consensus, the prevailing type of social solidarity, or the principles of social control. Instead it moves beyond such simple dichotomies towards a more genuine comparative historical typology. It is by means of such a typology that significant similarities and differences between social formations can be identified.

Throughout Bernstein's work there is continual resort to dyadic classificatory schemas. Perhaps some ardent Lévi-Straussian might well consider that these illustrate the universal tendency in the human mind to think in terms of conceptual categories framed in binary oppositions, but such categories, even if valid, do not necessarily provide an adequate heuristic basis for analysing historical change in different social formations. Bernstein argues that his classifications are not merely dichotomous, but dialectical. However, to assert this is not to demonstrate it.

The following are some examples of his dyadic classifications:

mechanical solidarity	organic solidarity
individualized mechanical solidarity	personalized mechanical solidarity
expressive order	instrumental order
positional control	personal control
position oriented families	person oriented families
restricted codes	elaborated codes
communal	individualized
bureaucratic dominance	therapeutic dominance
purity of categories	mixing of categories
sacred	profane
collection curriculum (strong classification and strong framing)	integrated curriculum (weak classification and weak framing)

Because he fails to utilize a theoretically constructed concept of either mode of production or social formation, Bernstein tends to operate with a very abstract formalistic set of categories which he proceeds to discuss in terms of their exemplification in different societies, inadequately defined. In the 'Classification and framing' paper, for example, he illustrates his various concepts with a comparison of different approaches to the curriculum in western Europe,

England, Scotland and the US without having clearly identified the common and contrasting features of these societies. There is, of course, nothing wrong with classifying, or with developing typologies, as such. But what differentiates one schema from another is the nature of the questions which inform a typology and the theoretical problems it seeks to resolve. Bernstein argues that his aim is to arrive at a theory of cultural transmission and its social basis in 'the distribution of power and the principles of social control' (1971a, p. 48). If this is the case he would need, as a first priority, a theoretical construction of his object: power structures, their social bases and the dynamics of their transformation. Without it, he finds it difficult to engage in a rigorous historical and comparative examination of the issues under discussion.

Bernstein has indeed addressed his attention to the issue of comparative sociology. He is right to regard much that passes under its guise as trivial and uninformative but his own account of what he means by 'constructive comparative research' does not enable us to proceed very far. We agree that it should be conducted on the basis of a 'problematic' rather than a 'low level specification of the problem' and that common research instruments have little to do with the basic issues (1975, p. 15). But the following quotation, read in conjunction with our earlier comments, illustrates the woolliness of his notion of 'problematic' and his failure to realize that comparative research requires some theoretical articulation and specification of the range of possible variation in the structures and processes under study:

> The (research) instrument destroys any possibility of understanding the form the problematic takes in different societies: indeed it ensures that the question is never the object of study. What I believe is required for basic comparative research is that the various groups adopt their own perspective on the problematic and within each perspective each group has the responsibility of creating procedures which can be made public and so subject to criticism. We might then have an understanding of how variations between societies shape the realization of the problematic. (1975, p.16).

Apart from the confusion revealed in this quotation between the notion of a theoretical problematic and a substantive issue to be resolved, there are a number of other difficulties. Given Bernstein's argument in the 'Class and pedagogies' paper, that educational transmissions embody class ideologies which are crucial to the cultural reproduction of class relationships, one would have expected the theoretical constitution of different forms of class relationships in the various social formations he considers to have been specified. It is perhaps significant that Bourdieu similarly lacks any clear articulation of his theoretical problematic which would permit a comparative historical dimension to be added to his work. He is frequently cited by Bernstein as sharing a similar preoccupation with the structure of symbolic reproduction, and their intellectual relationship referred to as exemplifying how comparative work can and should proceed. There is, however, little evidence that their collaboration is likely to lead to work of the quality of that of Eugene Genovese or Perry Anderson, where, through an extensive reading of the literature pertaining to different countries, and the use of a sophisticated theoretical framework, the contrasts and convergencies within and between different social formations have begun to be clarified (Anderson, 1976; Genovese, 1969).

Bernstein admits that the critical question, 'How do power relations penetrate into the organization, distribution and evaluation of knowledge through the social context' remains as yet unanswered. A necessary element of any possible solution to such a question would be a theory of ideology and of the process of hegemony, articulated with an analysis of how the state manages to maintain social cohesion whilst simultaneously guaranteeing the necessary preconditions for continued capital accumulation. Whilst, in his recent work, Bernstein has begun to utilize a concept of ideology, the specification of what is implied by such a notion is unclear. We would argue that his continual reference to the idea of social control and the principles which regulate social order is necessarily tied in with his structural-functionalist assumptions. In such a framework, social order is explained primarily in terms of normative control, an idea incompatible with a Marxist problematic. We shall elaborate below the importance of the Marxist concept of hegemony and the indissolubility of the idea of ideological control *and* coercion in the understanding of the maintenance of class dominance. Bernstein rarely invokes a concept of coercion, even though he frequently makes reference to the structural significance of differential power relationships in society. It necessarily follows from his Durkheimian starting point that he is more interested in relationships of authority. Moreover, when he admits that the ideological content of the different educational codes has been left out of the analysis, it is clear that he thinks of ideologies as sets of ideas rather than material practices embedded in rituals and routines. It is strange that he thinks that his discussion of the different social practices, procedures and routines which characterize the different educational knowledge codes, has little to do with ideology, especially given his view of their implications for power and authority relationships between teachers and taught, and potentially for macrosocietal features. We would suggest that a project which attempts to think through the structural and interactional levels of analysis requires a sophisticated theory of ideology for its success. Since individual subjects are constituted, at least, partly, within ideology (Althusser, 1971b) and since institutional structures are mediated and articulated through ideology, it is problematic for Bernstein to have relied primarily on Mead for the provision of a framework to understand interaction. Mead's perspective is fundamentally idealist, depending upon the individual knowing subject as the source of consciousness and meaning, and is incompatible with a view of ideology as material practice. We contend that a theory of cultural reproduction which locates the process of cultural transmission as its central focus cannot proceed very far unless that which is to be reproduced, and the role of ideology in the cultural reproduction process has been thought through with a greater degree of clarity than that provided by Bernstein's schema. Similarly, we suggest that his work on sociolinguistics suffers from the same deficiencies. Perhaps Volosinov's attempt (Volosinov, 1973) to provide a materialist theory of language or the recent attempts to integrate psychoanalysis with Marxism are more useful starting points. In both, language is seen as an important aspect of ideology (Coward and Ellis, 1977). The analysis of language as a sign system and the constitution of the subject within the unconscious structures of linguistic signs, within a historical materialist framework which locates class *relationships* as the context within which language is generated, provide a more fruitful framework.

The description and explanation of social change

Throughout Bernstein's work there is frequent reference to certain social processes occurring in societies which bring about social change. Despite the risk of overgeneralization, I shall attempt to summarize these in diagrammatic form. The exercise is difficult because the precise relationship between the various elements which are undergoing transformation are never clearly spelt out. Moreover, some of the causal sequences are occasionally reversed. For example, Bernstein argued (1975, p. 23): 'Class acts fundamentally on the division of labour by structuring its moral basis; that is by creating the underlying

51

relationships of production, distribution and consumption.' However, in much of his work on language changes in the division of labour itself are seen as responsible for transformations of the class structure.

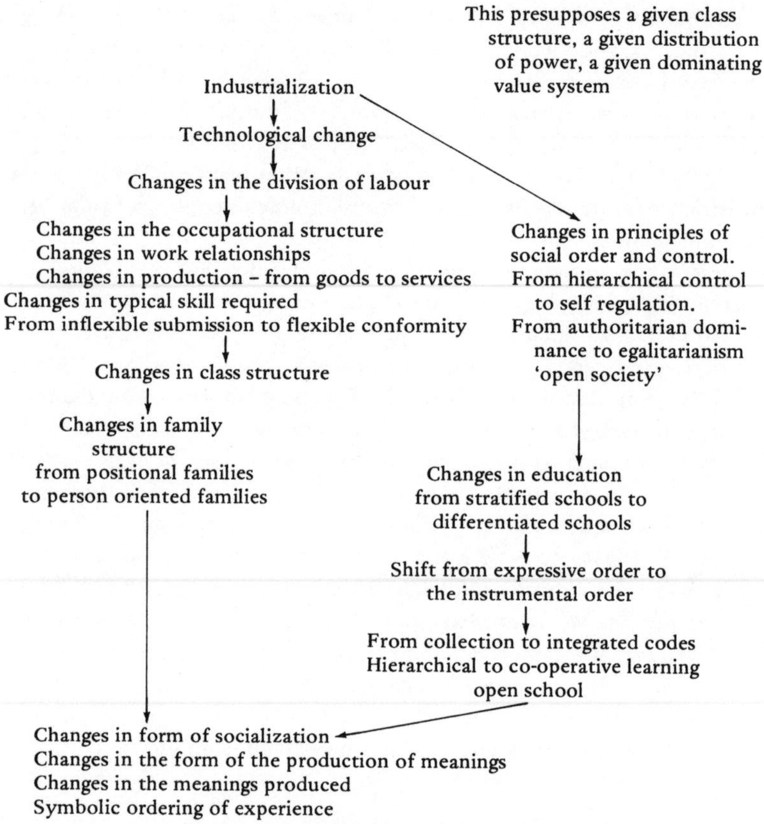

Industrialization
↓
Technological change
↓
Changes in the division of labour
↓

This presupposes a given class structure, a given distribution of power, a given dominating value system

Changes in the occupational structure
Changes in work relationships
Changes in production – from goods to services
Changes in typical skill required
From inflexible submission to flexible conformity
↓
Changes in class structure
↓

Changes in principles of social order and control. From hierarchical control to self regulation. From authoritarian dominance to egalitarianism 'open society'

Changes in family structure
from positional families
to person oriented families

Changes in education
from stratified schools to differentiated schools
↓
Shift from expressive order to the instrumental order
↓
From collection to integrated codes
Hierarchical to co-operative learning
open school

Changes in form of socialization ←
Changes in the form of the production of meanings
Changes in the meanings produced
Symbolic ordering of experience

Figure 3.1   Bernstein's model of social change

Despite some obvious lacunae, from this diagram it can be seen that Bernstein is basically using a structural functionalist framework, derived from Durkheim and Parsons, which emphasizes structural differentiation which emanates from the dynamic technological base of industrial societies. It is this which explains the shift from mechanical to organic solidarity. Until his most recent papers he has tended to postulate transformation within society from a relatively rigid hierarchical structure of domination to a more open flexible system embodying individualism, egalitarianism and plurality at the level of values. Such an optimistic orientation was typical of bourgeois social science in the 1950s and 1960s. It became more precarious and questionable only when the structural crisis of contemporary capitalism forced its way into public consciousness in the 1970s, even though Mandel and others have located the seeds of that crisis in the 1950s (Mandel, 1975).

Some may contend that this analysis of Bernstein's earlier work is unfair, given that he has always shown awareness of the fact of class inequality: the Marxist influence on his thought has been ever-present. We do not wish to deny his use of Marxist categories. What we would assert, however, is that the use of concepts like class inequality and class conflict does not, on its own, imply a historical materialist account of social classes and their role in social change. Bernstein's use of class categories will be discussed in the next section. It seems clear, however, from our previous discussion that he invokes a unidimensional concept of industrial society with its related ideas of technology and the division of labour as the key to understanding social change. He does not see the form that either technology or the division of labour takes to be a consequence not of industrial society *per se*, but of a *capitalist* mode of industrialization (Braverman, 1974; Brenner, 1977). He does not base his analysis of change in terms of a historical materialist account of the accumulation process and the class struggle as the antagonistic contradictory quality of the social relationships which comprise the social division of labour (Holloway and Picciotto, 1978). Indeed, he has never discussed industrial societies in terms of the contradictory processes built into the logic of capitalist development, given the social nature of production but the private basis of accumulation in the form of private property. Lacking such a framework, he analyses social change with what are little more than the descriptive categories of common sense. Consequently, none of the four reasons he cites for the movement from collection codes to integrated codes, are adequately explained. The four reasons are as follows:

1 the reorganization of knowledge at the higher levels;
2 the change in the demand for flexible occupational skills;
3 the movement towards greater egalitarianism requiring a more egalitarian education;
4 the problem of social control in advanced industrial societies which permit more pluralistic value systems.

These might seem, at one level, comprehensive. However, a number of issues arise. Why, for example, is there a change in knowledge at the higher levels and a process of increasing knowledge differentiation? How far is the social organization of knowledge a function of its appropriation by the bourgeois class rather than of anything intrinsic to the growth of knowledge itself? To what extent is the concept of skill ideologically defined? Is it accurate to suggest that current changes in the division of labour require a labour force attuned to the higher level of the principles of knowledge? Moreover there is no discussion of the issue of egalitarian education in terms of the obvious mystification involved. Indeed, in much of his work on language there is an underlying assumption that schools could be a means of producing, if not an egalitarian society, at least a greater degree of equality. (See especially his paper, 'A critique of the concept of compensatory education'.) Finally, when he argues that in 'advanced industrial societies which permit, within limits, a range of legitimizing beliefs and ideologies, there is a major problem of control' and that integrated curricula facilitate a new and more penetrating system of constraints, his explanation of the social control problem is located again in changing technology. He does not proceed to relate this to what he suggests is the more fundamental explanation for a shift towards integrated codes – that there is a crisis in society's basic classification and frames and therefore a crisis in its structures of power and control. It is the limitations of Bernstein's problematic and method that produce his incapacity to explain what a historical materialist would regard as a threat to the prevailing hegemony. Such hegemonic crises are periodically produced by the contradictory aspects of the accumulation process and the course of the class struggle. The 'unfreezing of the structuring of knowledge . . . to change the boundaries of consciousness' (1971) may be a necessary aspect of the process of maintaining or re-establishing hegemony. We maintain that the Marxist concepts of ideology and hegemony are essential for any analysis of the forms and processes through which knowledge is managed, and that the role of the state in the maintenance of hegemony is of critical significance in times of structural crisis in the capitalist mode of production. It is significant that the state is absent from Bernstein's theorizing, presumably reflecting its success in the process of achieving hegemony such that both its class basis, and its critical significance for the reconstitution of education in times of crisis remain hidden, even from Bernstein himself.

Bernstein's use of class categories

Let us begin by citing a few sentences in which Bernstein explains what he means by the concept of class.

> If a social group by virtue of its class relation, that is, as a result of its common occupational function and social status . . . (1971b)

> variations in behaviour found within groups who fall within a particular class (defined in terms of occupation and education) within a mobile society . . . (1971b)

From these quotations we can observe that Bernstein is utilizing a Weberian theory of social stratification. Modern societies are seen as hierarchically differentiated along the dimensions of class, status and power. When he refers to the fundamental importance of class inequality, what he basically means is that there is an unequal distribution of people's life chances, in terms of their access to income, occupation, education and status etc. Classes are defined in terms of a hierarchy of different groups with varying resources and prestige. His concept of class thus locates him clearly within the framework of bourgeois sociology (Sinha, 1977). In the latter we find a static empiricist differentiation of groups along a number of hierarchical dimensions which are theoretically unrelated to each other, their dynamic aspects unexplicated. Given this type of approach, explanations are often circular and tautological. For example, classes *defined* in terms of income and education, are often invoked as the reason why income and educational differentiation occurs.

It would not be fair to Bernstein to accuse him of expounding tautological explanations. For example, he has tried to identify what it is about some working-class families that produce variations in linguistic usage and hence contribute to educational failure. Nevertheless his approach varies considerably from a Marxist account of class which refers to relations of production within modes of production or social formations. He lacks a view of social classes in symbiotic *relationship* with each other within the social division of labour. Moreover, he sometimes discusses power as if it were conceptually distinct from class. For a Marxist, of course, class relations *are* relations of power, and power cannot be adequately discussed apart from a discussion of class relationships, in their economic, ideological and political aspects.

Bernstein's tendency to consider class in terms of superficial surface appearances rather than as a more fundamental structural category related to the social division of labour, can be seen in his account of the gradual demise of the typical working-class positional family. He provides the following reasons for the emergence of what he conceptualizes as a more personally oriented family structure (1971b):

1   Greater affluence, greater geographical mobility and, therefore, greater responsiveness to a wide range of influences which has been partly assisted by mass media.

2   Rehousing into areas of relatively low population density.

3   A change in the power position of the wife through her independent earning capacity.

4   A change in attitude both towards education and child development on the part of the working-class groups and therefore greater responsiveness to education and subsequent social mobility.

5   A change in the solidarity between workers arising out of, until recently, full employment and higher earnings.

6   A shift in the division of labour away from goods to that of a service economy. This is part of a long-term trend from goods to a service economy, an economy which is now more person than object oriented.

We do not deny that some of these empirical processes may have occurred, but it is important that they themselves should be explained. Bernstein does not deem it necessary to relate them to more fundamental dynamics in the movement of capital and its implications for changes in the social relations of production. There is no discussion, for example, of the breaking down of traditional working-class communities brought about by the geographical relocation of industrial production and changes in the labour process, of the role of the local state apparatus and capitalist building firms in the redevelopment of inner-city areas; neither is there any mention of the role of the state, mass media, and trade unions, in bringing about a partial ideological incorporation of the working class in conditions of rising wages and full employment, nor of the implications of a sudden reversal of that process in an economic crisis. In other words, he isolates changes within the working class from a consideration of the class relationship to the means of production and to other classes. Nor does he recognize the importance of ideology and politics in maintaining that relationship. Each factor is considered separately, the common roots unexplained.

The second example to illustrate his failure to discuss social class in a Marxist framework is in the 'Class and pedagogies' paper. Ironically Karabel and Halsey cite this as the main example of Bernstein's recent more thoroughgoing confrontation with Marxist categories. Here he is interested in the implications of the development of the 'new middle class' with its 'progressive' educational ideology, for the growth of an 'invisible pedagogy', particularly within the lower levels of schooling. The new middle class he identifies as developing in response to the shift away from entrepreneurial activities towards those occupations concerned with management, professional and other services. This is all connected to the process he mentions continually throughout his work of the relative decline in the production of goods compared with the production of services. In order to illustrate the characteristics of the new middle class it is necessary to cite a few quotations:

> It is clear that in advanced industrial societies, especially in the west, there has been a considerable increase in the division of labour of social control based upon the specialized modes of communication (symbolic control). This has created a vast range of occupations dedicated to the symbolic shaping and reshaping of the population. (1975)

> The basic fractions of the class that interested me were that fraction which reproduced itself through ownership and control over capital in its various forms, and that fraction which controlled not capital but dominant and dominating focus of communication, i.e. control over symbolic systems, over various forms of public education and symbolic markets. (1975)

> Personalized organic solidarity develops out of increases in the complexity of the division of labour of cultural or symbolic control which the new middle class have appropriated. (1975)

> [Property] has become partly psychologised and appears in the form of ownership of valued skills made available in educational institutions. (1975)

The emergence of this class is significant, Bernstein suggests, because it is associated with a change in the form of class reproduction characterized by a shift from individualized to personalized organic solidarity. Within the lower levels of education an invisible pedagogy has developed which, alongside the visible pedagogy of the old middle class, in practice discriminates against the working-class pupil. At the higher levels of schooling the invisible pedagogy gives way to a visible pedagogy. This alone, he believes, can translate educational capital into the form of private intellectual property, via the qualifications necessary for access to middle-class occupational roles. However, he considers that the invisible pedagogy of the integrated curriculum generates the potential for rendering visible the fundamental contradictions within society. One of these contradictions is experienced particularly by the new middle class:

> The new middle class, like the proponents of the invisible pedagogy are caught in a contradiction; for their theories are at variance with their objective class relationship.
>
> The contemporary new middle class are unique, for in the socialization of the young is a sharp and penetrating contradiction between a subjective personal identity and an objective privatized identity, between the release of the person and the hierarchy of class.
>
> The changes which are occurring, therefore, do not alter the *fact* of class reproduction, only the form. Neither is the separation of school from work overcome, nor can it be, in a class society.

We do not propose to discuss all the ideas in this paper. Bernstein admits that the paper is 'strange. It lacks the rather tight conceptual basis of the other essays. . . . There are a number of ideas which are not properly developed and they spill over into a series of notes at the end of the paper . . . I am well aware that the analysis is not under control; there are too many things going on.' We merely want to raise some issues regarding the way Bernstein conceptualizes the new middle class and point to some obvious difficulties, from a Marxist perspective, whilst recognizing that its lack of clarity has been accepted by Bernstein himself. He does, however, suggest that Bourdieu's work may provide the basis for further clarification, which, as will be suggested in the next section, is somewhat dubious.

First, the constant references to the shift in production from goods to services and its associated occupational implications, needs to be related to Marx's analysis of the tendency towards generalized commodity production where all use-values, including services, take the form of commodities, and to the explication of the circuit of capital in terms of the interrelated processes of production, distribution, and exchange. Bernstein himself, as we have seen, uses the terms production, distribution and consumption when discussing the effect of class on the division of labour but it is doubtful whether he has ever come to terms with the dynamics of capitalist production in terms of the various interrelated circuits of capital Marx outlines. This reminds us of the way he outlines Marx's theory in our earlier quotation. It is problematic from a Marxian viewpoint to talk of capital being 'manipulated and exploited' and to apply such terms to the issue of cultural capital.

Second, his analysis of the class position of the new middle class is thwart with difficulties. Now it would be foolish to deny that this is a difficult issue. It has recently been addressed by Poulantzas, Carchedi, Wright, among others, with a greater clarity than Bernstein's discussion provides. What the former agree upon is that the new petit bourgeoisie has to be analysed against a background of the process of concentration and centralization of capital, the differentiation of the functions of capital between different agents, and the differentiation and hier-archization of the collective labourer (Marx). It is difficult to talk about the new middle class as a homogeneous category. Elements of the new middle class perform some of the functions of capital. They often wield control over labour and over the allocation of investment priorities. Some members of the class perform ideological and political functions in the maintenance of hegemony. However, other elements are engaged in activities little different from those performed by working-class productive labourers. They are thoroughly proletarianized. It is imperative that any discussion of the new middle class should be conducted within the context of changes in the total social division of labour, and the political and ideological preconditions for the main-tenance of the capital relation.

A further problem with Bernstein's formulation is his discussion of knowledge or symbolic capital as private property, analogous to other forms of capital. Knowledge is, or can be, an important means of production, but that does not render those who 'own' the knowledge in their heads a separate fraction of the bourgeois class. Intellectual workers like journalists, teachers, university lecturers, those whom Bernstein cites as the controllers of symbolic capital, are often involved as wage labourers in the capitalist mode of production, employed by capital or by the state, and their knowledge appropriated by capital to serve class ends. Of course, there still are intellectual workers who are not wage earners, those who are engaged in petit bourgeois relations of production as independent commodity producers, but the long term tendency within capitalism is for such workers to become proletarian-ized. Large sections of the new middle class are involved in the function of the reproduction of labour-power (Althusser) as, for example, doctors, lawyers, teachers, or social workers, or in the reproduction of the means of production, as engineers, technologists, etc. Whilst there is an obvious difference between such workers and the bourgeoisie proper, it is important that their class location should be discussed in relationship to the development of the capitalist mode of production as a whole and to the necessary forms of its reproduction. In addition, capital remains a unitary structural position within class relations even if the functions of capital have become differentiated between different agents (Wright, 1976).

Since classes are constituted ideologically and politically as well as economically, it is important to clarify the changes in the class position of those in between the entrepreneurial categories and the proletariat, especially if the ideological implications of such changes is a matter of concern, as it is with Bernstein. Wright's attempt to do this provides a useful way of identifying subtle differentiations within the middle class in relationship to both the substantive and legal elements of capitalist control over the means of production and over labour-power. His perspective also provides a means for identifying possible class alliances and conflicts, and a useful way of thinking about the middle class in terms of their sometimes contradictory class locations. Bernstein's discussion of the ambiguous nature of their class identity and the contradictions they experience is far cruder and is not founded on a Marxist concept of contradiction. A perceived contradiction between a subjective self-identity as free and an objective reality of class hierarchies may be an index of more basic contradictions at the structural level, but these do need to be elucidated within the framework we have outlined. Although the contradiction Bernstein notes in the new middle class may be important in influencing class consciousness and class action, the structural preconditions for this need to be carefully theorized. It should not be forgotten that elements of the new middle class that Bernstein describes formed part of the social basis of fascism in Nazi Germany! (Poulantzas, 1974).

Bernstein tries to draw out some of the implications of collections and integrated knowledge codes for existing power and authority relations. However, many of his propositions depend upon somewhat contentious ideas which he does not spell out in detail. He suggests that education in depth as opposed to education in breadth is more likely to support an elitist monolithic class system (are these not ideological notions in themselves?) and that integrated codes have a greater potential for enabling people to see through the fundamental social contradictions and ambiguities – but these are hardly more than assertions. How would he explain, for example, the widespread crisis of hegemony occurring in western Europe, particularly among the educated intelligentsia, students, teachers, journalists, writers, etc., those who have been educated often to the highest levels and *not* via an integrated knowledge code? Similarly, what explanation does he provide for the absence of a genuine radical intellectual tradition in the US – a country which, surely, best exemplifies his concept of the integrated code? Again, how would he deal with the resurgence of a Marxist scholarship in the social sciences in Britain, a country which has traditionally provided one of his own examples of a collection code? We maintain that since Bernstein's classificatory schema is not thoroughly grounded in an analysis of the dynamics of the capitalist mode of production in different social formations he would have difficulty resolving these issues. Because he has no theory of ideology, he is incapable of under-standing the changing dynamics of class relationships in the context of the capitalist accumulation process and their underlying implications for the ideological role of schooling.

A further attempt by Bernstein to integrate his theoretical schema with Marxist categories is to be found in 'Aspects of the relations between education and production' (1977). An extended commentary on this chapter is justified both by the ambitious nature of the project and by its singular lack of success. Defining his aim as a consideration of 'the relationship between education and production, school and work' and noting that Gintis and Bowles, Althusser and Bourdieu 'do not give much space in their theorizing to change, conflict and contra-diction', he proceeds to apply his concepts of classification and framing to the 'codes of education and production' and their interrelationship. He sees both as emanating from the class structure, the forms of which vary historically, as also do the two codes. Both serve to reproduce class which he conceives of as the 'dominant cultural category, created and maintained by the mode of production'. Class 'creates the social re-lationships of production'. The latter he discusses in terms of their most basic unit 'at the level of the shop floor'. These basic relations of production vary in relation to the 'form of the productive act', i.e. 'what is made' and to the 'form of the relations between agents of pro-duction'. Whatever Bernstein means in this context by class, we should note the non-Marxist usage. Class relations are not seen as the social relations of production but as distinct relations determining the latter.

Neither are the social relations of production viewed as an essential part of the way the concept of mode of production is defined. Indeed, Bernstein does not explain what he means by the social relations of production, he only defines their basic unit in the way referred to above. The key concern in the chapter is both the 'dependent and relatively autonomous features of the relationship between education and production'. He argues that 'where there is a strong classification between education and production, this creates the conditions for the relative autonomy of education and thus a division of labour between those who are located in production and those who are located in cultural reproduction (education); that is, between power and control'. 'Strong classification' refers to a situation where 'work (production) and knowledge (education) are insulated from each other'. With reference to the relationship between the mode of education and the mode of production, Bernstein suggests that the question needs to be posed in terms of 'the form of regulation of the act of educational acquisition' (classification and framing) and 'the form of regulation of the act of production'; in other words in terms of the codes of education and production. Moreover, 'we must do this separately for different agents of production'. He sees the implications of the relationship between the two codes in terms of the reproduction of different types of consciousness, skills and dispositions. The unstartling conclusion follows:

> As soon as we consider in these terms the relationships between
> the mode of education and the mode of production under
> conditions of advanced capitalism, the more complex they become
> to unravel them in detail, although in general one can find at
> different levels a broad correspondence but also apparent
> contradictions.

The full significance of the term 'apparent' in this context is unclear. Nevertheless, we have moved full circle back to the original problem. To what extent are the concepts, classification and framing, codes of education and codes of production, helpful to its resolution? Bernstein suggests that 'In general, however, there is a correspondence between the dominant educational code (collection) and the dominant code of production, that is, between the strong hierarchically based classification of education and the strong hierarchically based classification of the modes of production'. However, he recognizes on the other hand that the movement towards a relaxation of classification and framing in the education of the less able child, and a similar more general shift in pedagogy in Sweden provides an indication of the relative autonomy of education or its relative independence from production. Nevertheless, he concludes: 'irrespective of the correspondences or contradictions between the regulation of the mode of education and the mode of production, the class basis of the social relationships of the division of labour is still reproduced', and that 'whatever the dominant educational code, the middle class are much more likely to possess the means of its appropriation and reproduction'.

At this point, we are now unclear as to the precise heuristic value of the concepts of classification and framing for clarifying the relationship between the modes of education and production. Despite the assertion in an ambiguous footnote which relates class to the social relations of production and education via the codes, *and* the relationship between education and production, it is not at all clear how they are related or to what social phenomena variations in the nature of the relationship are due. At this juncture, Bernstein introduces an additional category, that of 'systemic relations' between education and production. Re-iterating that education is a class allocating device which approximately reproduces the differentiated skills and dispositions required by the mode of production, he nevertheless asserts that 'education may and does create contradictions with reference to what is required by the class basis of the social relations of the mode of production', but not necessarily so in producing the appropriate 'distribution of', 'relations between' and 'expected realizations of' the 'categories required by the mode of production, he nevertheless asserts that 'education may and duction refer, thus, to the 'approximate reproduction of the work force.' They can be simple or extended, although we are given no criteria with which to make the distinction. We are also told that, despite variations in the systemic relations, the educational system maintains the 'dominating principle' of the social structure, which we have already learned is class. Furthermore, we are told that the systemic relations 'create for education the form of its economic or material base' and that 'they constitute both the class and the material basis of education'. This might be considered all very confusing. However, in the next sentence Bernstein reassures us somewhat: 'In as much as this is the case, this relation indicates the dependency of education on the mode of production. However, we shall also argue that education is relatively independent or relatively autonomous of production.' We are back to square one. So far, none of the concepts facilitate the analysis of to what extent, how, or why education is related to production.

Bernstein provides a few descriptive examples of situations of relative autonomy. In pre-industrial Europe, for example, he argues that education was subordinate to the church. In its fight to gain independence from the church, Bernstein argues that 'the autonomy of education was followed by the increasing dependency of education on the mode of production and, thus, on the state'. This quotation reveals the somewhat idiosyncratic nature of his definition of 'mode of production'. In a Marxist framework both the church and the state would have a location within the concept of mode of production and not outside it. His other examples relate specifically to capitalism and serve to undermine the correspondence thesis that the form and content of education relate directly to capital's requirements and that alone. No one would disagree with his observations but they are merely descriptive and do not assist Bernstein in the resolution of his main problem which is to *analyse* the relation between education and production.

At this point Bernstein reintroduces the concept of classification and asserts that the 'crucial relation between education and production is the strength of the classification between these two categories'. We are informed that 'where this classification is strong, then the principles, contexts and possibilities of education are not integrated with the contexts, processes and possibilities of production'.

Unfortunately, whilst this is framed in the form of a statement describing relationships, it is nothing but a tautology. We now have a definition of relative autonomy in terms of the 'strength of the classifications between the category education and the category production'. This is a slightly different formulation from that quoted earlier in which it was suggested that 'where there is a strong classification between education and production, this creates the conditions for the relative autonomy of education'. Thus the relative autonomy of education creates the conditions for the relative autonomy of education. Other clues concerning relative autonomy occur in the chapter, i.e. 'where education is not directly in rapport with a material base although it is affected by such a base' or where a social group differentiated from the ruling class, that is, 'those who dominate production by deciding its means, contexts and possibilities' had 'appropriated the form of educational transmission'. What is lacking, however, is any analysis of the conditions under which relative autonomy is generated. Instead we have nothing more than a descriptive statement that it sometimes exists. This will not do.

Having provided a definition of relative autonomy in terms of the strength of the classification between education and production, Bernstein then argues that this concept and the systemic relations between education and production can be used as the basis for classifying the 'structural relation' of education in different social structures. There are, he suggests, at least three possibilities:

(a) 'strong classification and simple systemic relationships' (nineteenth-century entrepreneurial capitalism).

(b) 'strong classification and extended systemic relationships' (twentieth-century capitalism).

(c) 'weak classification and extended systemic relationships' (China, Romania, Cuba).

We are not provided with the criteria used to allocate particular societies (modes of production?) within his typology, but we are informed that type (b) comprises societies with very different dominating cultural categories (class structures).

What can be gained from all this typologizing? At the end we discover that education has relative autonomy in some societies, but not in others; that some societies have an integrated production code, others a divisive one, and these variations are related to differences in class structure; and that 'we do have cases where there has been a radical change in the mode of production ($-C$) and so in the dominant cultural category, a major reduction in the autonomy of education, but no correspondence in the code of production and the code of education'. The major absences, however, are the concepts with which to resolve any of the why questions. Bernstein, on the other hand, believes this is not the case: 'our aim is to show that the analysis can be applied to societies with very different dominant cultural categories. We are also raising the question of whether there are any features of the relative autonomy of education in Western capitalist societies which apply to societies with very different dominating cultural categories but where education occupies a similar structural relation.' His own conclusion of this section of the chapter is as follows: 'Different contradictions arise out of differences between the classificatory and systemic relationships of education in different historical periods and in social structures with different dominating categories.' This is hardly more than a restatement of the original problem. It is clear that the concepts provided offer little of heuristic value in its resolution.

The difficulty is that Bernstein seems to act as if the systematic (and often not so systematic) juxtaposing of concepts can do his theoretical and analytical work for him. The point of typologizing is that theoretically informed concepts somehow assist in explaining significant relationships, but this does not seem to be the case in this chapter. Moreover, many of his concepts have vague and shifting referents. The chapter hovers between sentences of the utmost clarity, and those which are either meaningless, sometimes tautological, or impenetrable. It is these sentences which mask (or reveal?) Bernstein's confusion. The attempt to integrate somewhat transformed Marxist categories with his own in an essentially ahistorical typological description deprives the reader of any of their explanatory power. Without history, Bernstein will always find it difficult to apply his undoubtedly ingenious and often brilliant mind to the very questions he rightly isolates as significant. Parallels, partial approximations, correspondences and apparent contradictions, to use his own terms, between education and production do characterize their trajectory. The historical specificities of these relations deserve analysis. In particular, the contemporary lack of fit between aspects of child-rearing, forms of pedagogy, and changes in capital's labour requirements and the role of the state in the reconstitution of a more appropriate relationship, require further exploration.

Pierre Bourdieu

The cultural sociology of Bourdieu and his co-workers at the Centre de Sociologie Européenne in Paris has acquired a significant following among those seeking to establish a sociology of the curriculum. The recent publication in English of *Reproduction in Education, Society and Culture*, which is concerned with the forms and processes of cultural reproduction, has added to Bourdieu's reputation for providing a framework which is thought to elucidate the cultural role of schooling. In this section the main elements of this project will be summarized. We shall then raise some critical comments regarding the nature of Bourdieu's framework, arguing that it necessarily ignores a range of significant substantive issues which clearly enter into any analysis of the ideological role of schooling.

Symbolic violence

His theory of cultural reproduction is premised upon an assumption that societies are divided hierarchically into classes and that these class structures are maintained and legitimated by symbolic violence. He outlines his theory in a series of formal propositions which, he suggests, hold true for all class societies, although, in his own empirical work, the illustrations and evidence are usually drawn from contemporary France.

In his paper 'Symbolic Power' (1977) he states clearly that his intention is a synthesis between two different traditions. The first is the idealist approach of, for example, Lévi-Strauss and Saussure, in which symbolic systems are categorized as structuring phenomenal reality through their own internal structuring: symbolic systems are thus 'structured and structuring'. He wishes, however, to add a conception of symbolic systems as performing a political function, in the maintenance of class dominance, in the tradition of Marx and Weber. Thus 'symbolic systems fulfil their political function as instruments of domination as structured and structuring instruments of communication and knowledge.' Bourdieu then proceeds to show how their political function is fulfilled by actively concealing, or producing a 'misrecognition' of the class relationships of domination upon which their own symbolic power rests. This is achieved by an ideological legitimation of relations of inequality by making them appear natural, fair, immutable, and by justifying the particular location of individuals and groups within that social hierarchy. Moreover, given that symbolic power works, for people usually do not recognize the real unequal power relations on which it rests, it buttresses those relations and adds its own power to those relations of dominance, whilst simultaneously reproducing itself.

Bourdieu suggests that dominant symbolic systems, or, as he refers to them elsewhere, cultural capitals, are produced, distributed and consumed in a set of social relationships relatively autonomous from those which produce other forms of capital. A distinctive intellectual field exists, with its own logic and processes, its own institutional forms like the educational system, academic societies and journals; its own hierarchy, and ideology of independence and autonomy. Its existence is not independent of the class structure. However, there is a division of labour within the dominant class between those agents who possess political and economic capital, on the one hand, and those who have cultural capital on the other. He subdivides the dominant classes into fractions, and suggests that whilst the former are dominant, the latter have some measure of independence especially given their control over, for example, the educational system which is the major instrument of cultural reproduction. He therefore sees symbolic systems as 'doubly determined' by pressures emanating from the intellectual field on the one hand, and, on the other, by classes and class fractions whose interests are expressed by the form and content of symbolic power.

In Bourdieu's theory, symbolic power is the focus of a class struggle. In the same way that subordinate and dominant classes compete over the distribution of economic capital, so there is a struggle over how reality should be symbolically defined. These struggles take place either

> directly in the symbolic conflicts of everyday life or indirectly
> through the struggle waged by specialists in symbolic production
> (full time producers) in which the object at stake is the monopoly
> of legitimate symbolic violence – that is to say, the power to
> impose (and even to inculcate) instruments of knowledge and
> expression of social reality (taxonomies) which are arbitrary
> (but unrecognized as such). (p.115)

In other words, these are struggles within the intellectual field as such. Thus, 'the field of symbolic production is a microcosm of the struggle between classes', 'the struggle for the rewards specific to the autonomous field of ideological production automatically produces euphemized forms of the ideological class struggle' (p. 117).

Bourdieu summarizes his project as the search for the scientific laws which will reveal how economic capital is translated into symbolic or cultural capital. He regards symbolic power as a subordinate form of power, but very important in the necessary process of legitimating other kinds of power relations. He wishes to avoid what he defines as a crude Marxist approach which tries to reduce mechanistically all sets of ideas to class interests. He wishes to preserve the insight of structuralism and semiotics that symbolic systems can only perform political functions because they possess an inner logic and structure of their own. He also stresses the importance of establishing sociologically the structural conditions for the relative autonomy of ideas. The latter is the result of the relative independence of the producers and propagators of cultural capital from those social relationships in which other kinds of capital are controlled. There is, however, some degree of overlap: thus, 'the field of ideological positions reproduces in a transfigured form the field of social positions.'

How does he apply this theory to education? Bourdieu suggests that in a class society, education, necessarily, is a process of symbolic violence in that it involves the imposition of a 'cultural arbitrary' by an 'arbitrary power'. That is to say, the culture of the dominant class is defined as *the* culture: it designates what it means to be educated, and this is then transmitted through the educational system. Consequently, because other class cultures differ significantly from that of the dominant culture, the educational system tends to reproduce itself through the reproduction of the hierarchical distribution of cultural capital. Schooling is biased in favour of those who, by virtue of their class habitus, have already acquired, via a process of cultural osmosis, the appropriate dispositions, attitudes to language and the other preconditions for educational success. Moreover, because of its ideology of autonomy, egalitarianism and openness, the overall effect is for its real class function to be concealed. The power relations which lie behind and sustain it are misrecognized and thereby the process of cultural and social reproduction is achieved.

No overall appraisal of Bourdieu's work will be attempted here. As with Bernstein's work, it contains a range of interesting ideas which are well worth exploring. Of more significance is the adequacy of the framework for developing a theory of ideology which we regard as a necessary precondition for a theory of schooling.

Liberal theory in disguise

Bourdieu has often been described as a Marxist, for example, by Kennet (1973) and Davies (1976) and, less categorically, by Raymond Williams (1977a). However, despite his continual use of Marxian concepts such as social formation, class fractions, class struggle, and the appropriation of capital, and his preoccupation with the role of symbolic violence in the maintenance of class inequality, I want to argue that, like Bernstein, he is operating within a problematic largely defined by bourgeois sociology. His theory of educational selection for example, is little more than a theory of cultural deprivation. Kennet refers to the critique of Baudelet and Establet (1971) who suggest that he 'reproduces in his explanations what the school uses in *its* verdicts and sanctions; he has merely displaced the spontaneous explanations given by the school (inequality of gifts) to resite it in the family (social inequality)'. Whilst Bourdieu would deny that in any ultimate sense the working class are culturally deprived (they have their own equally arbitrary, universalizing, legitimating culture), he certainly views them as lacking cultural capital – i.e. that culture which is highly esteemed both by the dominant class and by the institutions of schooling, and the power to impose their own culture on their offspring within the school. In other words, he sees schools as arenas where cultural differences come to be defined as cultural deprivations. But this theory is inadequate as a total explanation of what is occurring within schooling. What is needed is a more thorough analysis of the *context* of schooling which Bourdieu's approach fails to provide. Apart from asserting that there are social classes and asymmetrical power relationships, we learn little more about how the context of schooling should be theorized, let alone understood.

Moreover, with respect to those aspects of the context that he *does* discuss, i.e. the class structure, his approach is seriously deficient in generating significant insights. His apprehension of the class structure is through class categories firmly embedded within bourgois ideology. Like Bernstein, he does not conceive of social classes in terms of the social relationships of production, but rather as a complicated hierarchy of occupations. Incumbents of these occupations vary in their incomes and consumption habits and in the social prestige accorded to them. In his paper 'Cultural reproduction and social reproduction' (1973), for example, we find the different fractions of the dominant class defined according to the criteria of occupation. These fractions are seen to coincide with the socio-professional categories of the I.N.S.E.E. (the French equivalent of the Registrar General's classification of occupations). They include the following: (1) teachers; (2) administrators in the public sector; (3) members of the liberal professions; (4) engineers; (5) managerial staff in the public sector; (6) industrial employers; (7) commercial employers. How simple analysis would be if the different fractions of the ruling class could be so clearly identified! (Clarke, 1977). In the same paper he produces tables which appear to show that those whom he categorizes as the economically dominant fractions have the same incomes as those culturally dominant (teachers!). He elsewhere defines the dominant economic fractions as the owners of economic capital, but from his exposition it is clear that he is referring to those who have the highest income. For example, in the same paper he suggests that doctors and lawyers have high amounts of both cultural and economic capital. Now, whilst members of the liberal professions may have high incomes, they certainly do not usually constitute members of the capitalist class, from the point of view of a Marxist problematic. It is clear that he has no conceptualization of capital as involving both social and technical relations with respect to legal ownership and possession of the means of production. Similarly, in 'Reproduction', he refers to the working, middle and upper classes, but these are again defined in terms of occupation and social status. In addition, he has no concept of economic capital as something which does not necessarily accrue to individual agents, but to such institutions as banks, insurance companies, or large corporations. In the light of the criteria he uses for differentiating between different fractions of the dominant classes, it seems evident that he is really discussing occupational elites and not class fractions in the Marxist sense at all. A Marxist would differentiate fractions in terms of different types and sub-types of capital (money, commodity and productive capital) and in terms of their location in the circuit of capital, realized either within one social formation or cross-nationality.

Furthermore, although he makes frequent reference to the class struggle, he thinks of it as taking place in the market place. Distributional struggles over the allocation of the economic product in the form of goods or incomes derive from a neo-Ricardian, not a Marxist problematic. He does not seem to see class struggles as in any way related to the organization of production. Indeed, he makes scarcely any reference to the way production is structured and the social division of labour founded therein. Neither does he provide any tools for analysing the economic, political and ideological conditions within which class struggle is generated and waged. This derives from a further difficulty: the formalism and ahistorical nature of his theory. Whilst some might argue that the formal nature of his categories permit the possibility of comparative and historical analysis, in the absence of adequate theorization regarding the context of symbolic violence and its processes, it is difficult to see how comparative of historical analysis could be possible. With class defined, for example, in purely occupational terms, we have no means of discerning different types of class structure in different social formation, or the changing balance of class forces in different historical periods. Similarly, because he does not see social formations is being constituted by different modes of production which may be characterized by very different mechanisms of social and cultural reproduction, he is forced to make a whole series of formalistic propositions which are devoid of content and reveal very little potential for the understanding of the dynamics of social change.

This is singularly unfortunate, if only because in one of Bourdieu's earliest works on Algeria (1962), written at the time of the Algerian war, he showed himself acutely sensitive to the economic and political context within which cultural processes are generated and function. There he suggested cogently that aspects of culture like ethnic and racial prejudice, and the destruction of traditional Algerian cultural patterns should be analysed within the context of a theory of imperialism and economic exploitation. Since cultural reproduction is never automatic or guaranteed, such a historical and structural dimension to the theory is indispensable.

Social and cultural reproduction

It is now appropriate to consider Bourdieu's theory of social reproduction, which he defines as the reproduction of the relations of force between social classes. This is achieved, at least partly, by the reproduction of the cultural symbols which legitimize and thus sustain other relations of dominance. Just as economic capital is transmitted through the generations via the inheritance laws, so cultural capital is transmitted through the habitus in a way which confirms and reproduces the class structure.

Bourdieu's theory of reproduction differs significantly from a Marxist account. The latter would not only be concerned with the reproduction of a system of class relationships but with the reproduction of all the conditions for capital accumulation, at least in a capitalist society. It is not simply agents who have to be reproduced, as workers or as capitalists with the appropriate dispositions and motivations, but also the material and other means for reconstituting the capitalist production process. Mandel (1968), following Marx's schema as outlined in the three volumes of *Capital*, specifies three conditions which have to be satisfied for the reproduction of the productive system:

1 The production of capital goods which have to replace those consumed in the course of production, and consumer goods needed to reconstitute labour power.
2 The creation of purchasing power capable of realizing the value of those capital and consumer goods, and the spending of the same.
3 The distribution of purchasing power in such a way that the supply and demand balance as regards both capital and consumer goods.

Mandel argues that the study of reproduction must be grounded within an analysis of the economic preconditions for the reproduction of capitalist production. If the above conditions are not satisfied, the continuity of capitalist production is broken. Their analysis depends upon an understanding of the dynamics of the circuit of capital, through its various stages and forms. In addition, reproduction also involves the reproduction of a class relationship in which economic, political and ideological variables are involved. Accumulation takes place within definite class relations and is characterized by class struggle which can affect the necessary elements of capitalist reproduction.

Now although Bourdieu talks about the reproduction of a class structure, he does not discuss that process at all in the context of the dynamics of capitalist accumulation. Like most bourgeois social scientists, he, no doubt, relegates the economy to economists. We would argue, on the contrary, that cultural reproduction occurs within a context which itself is subject to a dynamism which needs to be theorized in order to comprehend the kind of issues with which Bourdieu is concerned. Moreover, the role of the state is central to any process of social and cultural reproduction. Bourdieu defines the state in Weberian terms, as the institution with the monopoly on legitimated violence but apart from several mere mentions of its existence, it does not enter into his framework at all. We will clarify in the next chapter the vital part the state plays in a Marxist account of cultural reproduction. Bourdieu enters into no discussion of the class basis of the state, its illusory autonomy from the mechanisms of civil society, nor of its central role in producing hegemony.

The discussion so far has concentrated on Bourdieu's method of analysis and the way in which he defines the problem. We have tried to show how Bourdieu is not working from historical, materialist assumptions and consequently how his framework omits a range of social phenomena which must be regarded as crucial elements of a theory of ideology. It is perhaps significant that Bourdieu's own discussion of a Marxist approach to ideas seriously misrepresents Marx's position. In 'Symbolic power' he suggests that 'the Marxist tradition gives preeminence to the political function of symbolic systems to the detriment of their logical structure.' He characterizes the Marxist theory of ideology in the following way:

> This functionalism . . . explains symbolic productions by relating
> them to the interests of the dominant class. In contrast to myth,
> which is a collective product collectively appropriated and
> consumed, ideologies serve sectional interests which they tend to
> present as universal interests common to the group as a whole.

73

> The dominant culture contributes to the effective integration of
> the dominant class (by making possible immediate communication
> between all its members and distinguishing them from other
> classes). It also contributes to the bogus integration of the society
> as a whole, and therefore to the demobilization (i.e. false
> consciousness) of the dominated classes. (p. 114)

This is a serious misrepresentation. The Marxist tradition has moved
beyond the reduction of ideologies to simple lies and capitalist plots
which obscure the real underlying structure of class relationships,
through the imposition of the ideas of the dominant class on to the rest
of the population who consequently suffer from false consciousness.
Whilst there may have been elements of that approach in *The German
Ideology*, even there Marx was adamant that the root of ideology lies
in the structure and processes of civil society. For example, his whole
critique of classical political economy is framed in terms of an examination and critique of the structures of capitalist society in which such
a system of ideas is generated. In *Capital*, moreover, the idea of commodity fetishism provides the basis for a much more sophisticated
understanding of ideology, as representations of a reality, the world of
appearances, which is in every way as real as the structure of the deeper
connections it hides. It also provides a way of thinking about ideology
in relation to the movement of capital which, as we have seen, Bourdieu
fails to do. In this respect, he is merely following a long tradition of
French structuralists (including so-called Marxists), who, in their
concern to develop an analysis of the relatively autonomous level of
ideology, have managed to separate it, conceptually and analytically,
from the other levels of the structure of the social formation, to the
detriment of their final explanations.

However, Bourdieu might well respond that he has at least provided
an account of the historical and social conditions which facilitate the
development of a relative autonomy and independence of cultural or
symbolic systems. He suggests that 'all influence and constraint exercised by an authority outside the intellectual field is always refracted
by the structure of the intellectual field', which is both determined and
determining. He writes:

> As the areas of human activity become more clearly differentiated,
> an intellectual order in the true sense, dominated by a particular
> type of legitimacy, began to define itself in opposition to the
> economic, political and religious powers, that is, all the authorities

who could claim the right to legislate on cultural matters in the name of an authority which was not properly speaking intellectual. (Davies, 1971, p. 162)

He locates this period at the end of the Renaissance when 'the intellectual field [is] becoming increasingly independent of external influences (which from this point on must pass through the mediating structure of this field)'. This field is 'governed by a specific logic: competition for cultural legitimacy' (a neo-Ricardian struggle over culture?). Whilst there are many exciting insights generated from his discussion of the intellectual field, Bourdieu fails to provide any concepts for analysing the crucial issue, which is what determines which external influences manage to penetrate within its boundaries and which do not. In this connection, Bourdieu's work is closely akin to Weber's discussion of status groups like the Chinese literati, their role being considered in relative isolation from the differentiation of the social formation in terms of social classes defined in terms of the social relations of production.

We shall argue that, certainly with regard to the situation in contemporary capitalist societies, the form and content of cultural capital is centrally related to the nature of bourgeois society and the balance of class forces within it. Bourdieu, on the other hand, seems to believe that if a differentiation can be established within the dominant classes between agents who possess cultural capital and those who possess other forms, then this necessarily implies a degree of autonomy. However, as has been suggested, the unity of a class is not itself undermined by a division of labour between different agents. The prevalence of bourgeois ideology even in social formations where the effective political dominance of the bourgeois class seems threatened (Italy, France, Spain) bears witness to this, as also does the nature of Euro-communism.

In conclusion, whatever the nature of the language which Bourdieu employs to articulate his theories, his framework is fundamentally a Weberian one. We should beware of the historic tendency of hegemonic classes to incorporate potentially counter-hegemonic movements within the framework of assumptions of the dominant ideology. In the last few years, there has been a resurgence of interest in Marxism among social scientists and other intellectuals in western capitalist societies, coinciding with the restructuring crisis in the world capitalist system. Bourdieu's work illustrates the tendency to incorporate some Marxist categories whilst simultaneously defusing their most radical potential.

That radical potential rests upon Marx's insight that right at the heart of capitalist production processes there lies a fundamental contradiction related to two features: the social nature of production and the private basis of accumulation; the contradiction between use value and exchange value. This insight need not commit us to any 'inevitable breakdown' theory. It should, however, lead us to a search at the theoretical level for the potential fissures both in bourgeois ideology and in bourgeois society in order to ground an appropriate political practice. Bourdieu's work fails to do that, and in that respect he provides yet another illustration of the appropriation of bourgeois social science, even under a radical guise, by the bourgeois class.

Michael Young

Michael Young's work differs from that of either Bernstein or Bourdieu in that it is less obviously an exercise in pure theory. Young's sociology of education is self-consciously moral and political. Its social roots are to be located in the late 1960s, in Britain's growing economic, social and political problems, illustrated at both the political level by the crisis in social democracy and within theory by the growing criticism of a reformist approach to educational issues represented by Fabianism (Finn, Grant and Johnson, 1977). The crisis increasingly brought the subject of the curriculum to the fore, which, according to Young, had been accepted as an unproblematic 'given' in earlier sociological discussions of education. Along with others (Davies, 1969; Bernstein, 1971) Young defined his task as the reorientation of the discipline away from its central preoccupation with stratification, 'narrowly conceived', towards the management of knowledge as the key substantive issue.

His work falls into three main stages. The first can be characterized by his attempt to produce a sociology of the curriculum in his course for postgraduate students at the London Institute of Education, which culminated in the publication of *Knowledge and Control* (1971), a collection of papers by various authors including one of his own: 'An approach to the study of curricula as socially organized knowledge'. This collection set out to define 'new directions in the sociology of education'. In the second period, influenced largely by Mead and Schutz, he was preoccupied with the exploration of teachers' and others' typifications of key educational categories like 'knowledge', 'ability', 'science' in such interaction settings as classrooms and the

Schools Council. Third, in his more recent writings, he has reverted to more macrosociological concerns and their implications for a radical educational practice. What gives each of these stages their essential unity is his political stance, implicit in his earlier work, but formulated explicitly in recent papers as the search for a socialist society in which 'man's common humanity could be realized' (Young *et al.*, 1976, p. 2).

Stage 1 1967-71: An outline for a sociology of the curriculum

The key theme in his earlier work is the necessity of rendering problematic what counts as educational knowledge. Despite the claims of educators that the knowledge they teach is 'objective', Young argues, on the contrary, that all knowledge is 'socially, and historically constructed' or 'situated' (1973), relative to a particular time or social context. What counts as an educational curriculum involves a particular selection and organization from potential available knowledges. A curriculum has no essential validity: it merely reflects a particular distribution of power in society which produces the differentiation and stratification of knowledge characteristic of educational curricula. Thus:

> It may be through this idea of the stratification of knowledge that we can suggest relations between the pattern of dominant values and the distribution of rewards and power and the organization of knowledge. Such analysis would be necessary both historically and cross-culturally on the societal level, and also at different age levels and different knowledge areas. (1971a, p. 31)

The 1971 paper makes no pretence of resolving all the significant issues. It reviews, rather, a range of approaches and studies pertaining to both the social structural and interactional dimensions, posing significant problems and attempting to clarify the areas where further thought and research is required. It is self-consciously eclectic. Young suggests that: 'sociological research drawing on the Marxist, Weberian and Durkheimian traditions can contribute to a reorientation of the sociology of education, that would no longer neglect curricula nor . . . conceive of it as an epiphenomenon' (p. 31). Although he provides only ambiguous directions for future theoretical development, at this stage, there is an essentially modesty about what had so far been achieved and what questions still remain open. He recognizes the 'lack of an overall framework for linking the principles for the selection of content to the social structure,' admitting that 'we do not know how the relations between the economy and the educational system produce different degrees and kinds of stratification of knowledge' (p. 40). In addition, he confesses that the concepts with which to link the social structural dimensions with organizational and interactional processes are lacking: 'our understanding of this process is so rudimentary at present that it is doubtful if we can postulate any clear links between the organization of knowledge at the level of social structure and the process as it involves teachers in the classroom' (p. 32). Nevertheless, the paper should be read as an important initial contribution to the debate about the content of educational knowledge.

There are, however, some serious difficulties in Young's position, from a Marxist perspective, which relate to some continuing absences in his mode of theorizing. Young maintains that from his viewpoint 'the sociology of education is no longer conceived as an area of enquiry distinct from the sociology of knowledge' (1971a, p. 3). We have suggested in our discussion of Mannheim the significant differences between the sociology of knowledge and a Marxist account of ideology, and the superiority of the latter problematic for an analysis of the link between knowledge, ideology and schooling. Given Young's concern with power relationships and their implication for the stratification of knowledge in the curriculum, it is questionable to argue that the sociology of knowledge provides a central perspective, since the latter has not produced an adequate theory either of social stratification or of power relationships, both of which Young admits play a vitally important role. His own views on stratification and power depend heavily on an eclectic mixture of Weberian, Marxist and conflict theoretical concepts which are not specified with any rigour. He asserts, for example, a relationship between what he calls the 'dominant institutional order' and the organization and stratification of knowledge, but the former concept is, essentially, woolly; thus 'the dominant institutional order' is seen as the 'various economic, political, bureaucratic, cultural and educational interest groups that make up that order. . .'. A *theory* of stratification has to go beyond a mere description of different interest groups or a recognition that societies are divided hierarchically according to 'the distribution of rewards in terms of wealth, prestige and power'. It must be able to account for these differences and their relationships and their changes over time. A similar argument has been put forward with respect to Bernstein and Bourdieu and the suggestion made that a historical materialist focus on all aspects of the changing social relations of production provides greater access to the dynamic dimension of power relationships in social formations and to the role of ideology in their reproduction. Young might have found such an approach useful, given the relationships he tries to establish between different types of societies and the degree of independence of their respective educational systems. He states:

> It is possible to trace schematically a set of stages from non-literate societies where educational institutions are not differentiated from other institutions, to feudal-type societies where formal education in separate schools is almost entirely restricted to a priestly caste, and, through church ownership of land, such schools remained largely independent . . . of the economic and political processes of the time. Gradually schools and colleges became increasingly differentiated and dependent on the economies of the societies they were in, when clearly the dominant economic and political orders became the major determinants of the stratification of educational knowledge. (p. 40)

He proceeds to make a plea for comparative studies of educational arrangements in 'developing countries' to shed light on these connections. Apart from his tendency to separate economics from politics in a fetishized way (Clarke, 1977), and in spite of his use of the essentially bourgeois concept of 'developing' countries, it is clear that the employment of a Marxist periodization of history in terms of different types of modes of production and their varying forms of reproduction in different social formations would have been apposite. He would not have been able to argue that religion had little to do with the reproduction of feudal relationships of production and that feudal schools were more independent of economic and political forces than schools which exist in modern industrial societies.

Young's aim to relate, historically and comparatively, issues of power and social stratification to the organization of educational knowledge, requires a theory of ideology but this is not forthcoming from the various contributors to the sociology of knowledge which he discusses. It is again significant to examine his interpretation of Marx's analysis of ideas. He describes the Marxist tradition in terms of 'its focus on how knowledge is controlled and legitimated and its neglect of the equally important process of its acquisition' (1971a, p. 28). Whilst it is true that Marx never accounts satisfactorily for the mechanisms whereby agents become inserted into ideology as subjects,

Young seems to believe, like Bourdieu, that Marx's concept of ideology refers simply to ruling-class lies. He describes Marx as thinking of education as a 'tool of ruling class interests' and that 'it follows that the dominant emphasis of the educational systems of capitalist society which may be described as the competitive concern with exams, grades and degrees can be seen as one expression of the principles of a market economy' (p. 28). In the light of this, Young concludes that 'Whilst those ideas may be fine up to a point, they are on such a general level as to make them of limited value as starting points for the analysis of elite curricula' (p. 28). Apart from the distortions involved in this representation of Marx's account of ideology, in which the theory of commodity fetishism is completely ignored, Young appears to employ precisely the theory he has criticized in his own discussion of the way dominant power groups impose their own values and definitions of the good and the true on subordinate groups with different cultural conceptions. Whilst he mentions, approvingly, Gramsci's concept of hegemony (Gramsci, 1971), he does not utilize it in his own framework. An idea of powerful groups *imposing* their ideas on others is far from a notion of hegemony. An approach to the sociology of the curriculum which does not give equal emphasis to the forms and social practices involved in the transmission of educational knowledge has failed to develop the heuristic potential of the Gramscian concept of hegemony. Young's position seems to invoke a conspiracy theory of ideas as the means for explaining the stratification of knowledge in the curriculum. The concept of hegemony surely implies a fundamental continuity between what Young calls common sense, or everyday knowledge and the content of highly valued knowledge. Young seems to suggest basic discontinuity when discussing the involvement of the working class in the curriculum, whereas Gramsci certainly recognized the extent to which hegemonic beliefs and practices penetrated and moulded, at least partially, the content of common sense. He also tied in his analysis of hegemony with a consideration of the role of the state, a dimension which is significantly absent from Young's analysis.

A further difficulty with Young's emphasis on the stratification of educational knowledge, which results from his failure to theorize adequately the context within which the educational system works and from the lack of a rigorous theory of ideology, has been raised by Ahier (Ahier, 1977). The latter maintains:

> Following his criticism of the structural functionalist notion that
> some knowledge has high status because it is needed by society,

he is forced by the logic of conventional criticisms of this theory into believing that if this organization of the knowledge were upset, then there would be massive redistribution of the labels 'education', 'success' and 'failure' and thus also a parallel redistribution of rewards in terms of wealth, prestige and power.

Ahier throws doubt on the radical implications to be derived from the kinds of changes in social meanings in education which Young seems to be advocating. He accuses Young of being naive and operating too much within an educationalist's perspective, too preoccupied with 'those who rely on a particular kind of knowledge to distinguish themselves from the proletariate, i.e. the petit bourgeoisie'. He further maintains that Young is articulating an idealist view of the relationship between education and the structure of inequality within society. We will further explore this idealism in the context of the second period of Young's development.

Stage 2 1971–6: the social construction of reality

In his papers written in this period (1972, 1973a, 1973b, 1975a, 1975b, 1976a, 1976b) despite the frequent references to the political character of educational knowledge and the way structural factors impinge upon interaction, the concern with macrosocietal issues has receded into the background. Instead, we find Young preoccupied with how groups, through negotiation, within interaction, 'collectively order their world and produce knowledge'. Using concepts derived from Mead, Schutz and ethnomethodology, he still wishes to define knowledge as problematic, but it is at the microlevel of interaction that he wishes to explore the processes involved. More explicitly than in his earlier work the concern is now to produce a 'sociology of education relevant to teachers' which therefore has to 'start with classroom practices and on those who produce constraints' (1975b). Similar themes appear in all the papers of this period: by investigating members' 'accounts' and their typifications of knowledge, ability, childhood, school subjects, etc., it will be possible to discern the 'constructed nature of what we have come to call formal bodies of knowledge or disciplines and enable us to see them like the knowledge reported by ethnographers, as the ongoing accomplishment of members.' (Young et al., 1976a). The rationale for doing so is that, if we can discern the historically contingent character of what counts as knowledge, we will be more able to see the possibilities for its redefinition. Thus: 'This potential resides in man's common humanity, his often unrealized capacity for changing as well as making his world' (Young *et al.*, 1976, p.2).

Young recognizes that his attack on the objectivity of the knowledge taught in schools raises the issue of relativism: the grounds of validity of his own, or anyone else's knowledge, but the problem does not unduly worry him. Since all knowledge is a social construction, we are forced epistemologically into relativism but, as actors in the world, we cannot be. He invokes the existentialist wager (Merleau-Ponty, 1969) and argues for commitment and responsibility.

It is the work of this period that has justly received the most trenchant criticism. (Pring, White, Whitty, Bernbaum, Simon, Banks, Inglis, Ahier, Karabel and Halsey, Sharp and Green, Demaine). Some elements of the critique are overstated, since they apply more to Young's followers (Esland, Keddie, Gorbutt, Bartholemew, Jenks) than to Young himself. Nevertheless, it seems not too unfair that he should share some of the responsibility for the excesses of his followers, since they were all at one time his pupils and some of them his co-authors.

Since the work of this period has been thoroughly appraised from a variety of perspectives by the authors mentioned above, it is not necessary to do more than summarize the three issues in the critique which are most pertinent from a Marxist viewpoint.

The first relates to Young's views on the mechanisms of cultural and hence social reproduction. His emphasis on the way the social meanings of educators sustain a particular set of unequal, hierarchical social relationships involves their separation from the material base in which they are generated and sustained (Demaine, 1977). Moreover, as Banks points out (1974), it appears to render school teachers and others who impose knowledge primarily responsible for the existence of social inequality in general, and educational inequality, in particular. Such a view entails an extremely naive explanation of social inequality and the role of ideology in its reproduction. As we have suggested above, a Marxist theory of ideology refers to more than mere mystification. Ideology also reflects a situation of substantive domination and its understanding depends additionally on a theory of the role of the state and coercion in the maintenance of dominance relationships, including dominance through ideas. We are, in other words, constrained by more than mere concepts (Sharp and Green, 1975).

The second and related element of the critique concerns Young's cultural, rather than political, radicalism. We have already referred to Ahier's comments in this regard. Young seems to be implying, Ahier maintains, that social equality can be brought about by transforming our social meanings and typifications. For example, if, in education, we redefine knowledge, eradicate the stratifying components and transform our pedagogy, then equality would follow. Now, at one level, of course, changes in knowledge have to precede any radical transform-ation of existing power structures, but Young is singularly vague on what sort of changes in knowledge are required, especially those which might inform effective political strategies. Young's cultural radicalism is tied in with an essentialist notion of the human subject. He advocates a romantic, humanist, individualism which prescribes an 'engagement in our history' (Young, 1973b) for a realization of 'human betterment' and 'our common humanity'.

The third element of the critique concerns his failure to come to grips with the relativistic implications of his ideas. In the discussion with White, for example, he continually sidesteps the issue, reiterating that the criteria for truth and validity are social, not 'given' in know-ledge, and not independent from the social group of 'knowers'. Young maintains that we should not 'ask whether particular research methods are good or bad but ask for what and for whom we are providing accounts' (Young, 1973, p.221). However, differences between theories are not just a question of social convention or who propagates or benefits from the belief. Despite the obvious difficulty of how we could even answer the above question without some validating criteria, and whilst in the last analysis, of course, theories are never finally supported or refuted by factual evidence, only replaced by other theories, that does not mean that all thought is arbitrary and that all we are left with is our own existential commitments (Young, 1975a). After all, we do need some way of distinguishing between people's commitments, their varying views of how the world is constituted, and their implications for action. Mussolini and Gramsci were both committed in different ways. Young seems to suggest that there is no way of judging between them.

Young's relativism in this period prevents him from realizing the potential of his approach to the sociology of the curriculum, in that he offers no grounds for accepting his ideas, rather than those of people like Peters and Hirst, whom he is criticizing. However, in some rather imprecise way, he does discern that the criteria of rationality, and hence validity, are in some way tied in with the idea of human betterment (Young, 1975c). Habermas's idea of communicative com-petence and the analysis of systematically distorted communication might have helped him to clarify his thoughts in this regard (Habermas, 1970).

In short, we feel that Young's work in this period offers little purchase on what we regard as the key substantive issue, that of the role of ideology in social reproduction. To be fair to Young, he also recognizes the inadequacies of this stage of his work and argues for a re-orientation.

Stage 3 1976 to the present: towards a radical political practice

Recently, Young has backpedalled from his previous commitment to social interactionism and phenomenology and has asserted the need for forms of political radicalism based upon an implicit diagnosis of the consequences of capitalism. In Young and Whitty (1977a) he writes of his own previous work and that of others in 'The New Sociology of Education': 'The implication to teachers [that] to suspend their own taken for granted assumptions and to examine critically their own practices, would produce a transformation in their activities was ludicrously naive.' It was naive because 'there are limits to people's possibilities for action'. Similarly, 'A theoretical critique of the necessities of hierarchies in education may be exciting in a seminar but is not any good to those who experience such necessities as real in practice' (Young, 1975a). He now recognizes that the constraints on both action and cognition relate to the very nature of capitalist society itself. Thus: 'The practices which keep society going and hide the ideological dimensions of prevailing views of knowledge from public view are not just those of the classroom but take place within a context as wide as capitalist society itself' (Young and Whitty, 1977a). 'Curriculum as fact is not mere illusion. It should be seen as a historically specific reality expressing particular production relations among men' (1975a). He also accepts that the new sociology of education has tended to be ahistorical and has 'failed to fulfil its promise'.

Despite the recognition of constraints, Young now believes that the main problem is to try to find a way between 'naive optimism and fatalistic pessimism' (Young and Whitty, 1977a). He criticizes Bowles and Gintis (1976), Althusser (1971b), and to a lesser extent, Sharp and Green (1975) for implying that, since education is essentially involved in class reproduction, there is nothing that radical teachers can do. He recognizes that 'educational strategies are limited in that they also involve changes in the relations of production' (1975b). However, since educational institutions are seen as the site of social contradictions which can be exploited, then radical initiatives among teachers are both possible and desirable. Entailed in this is the need to 'explore the institutional practices which produce and sustain the constraints within which teachers work' (Young and Whitty, 1977a) and the 'forging of collective alliances with others over wider political and economic issues'. What is required, he suggests, is a 'cultural critique of that society' and the 'creation of the elements of a genuine socialist future'. Working towards a wider definition of what counts as education and pedagogy would be part of this general strategy.

Young is correct to argue against the kind of superstructural determinism to which Althusser's position leads. The contradictions of the social relations of production are reproduced within the apparatuses of the state which are themselves significant sites of class struggle. What remains problematic, however, about Young's recent work, is still the nature of the context within which education works and plays its role. We now know that it is capitalist and that the social relations of production structure its main parameters, but beyond this, we are offered few clues as to what its inner dynamics are, where to locate the potential contradictions, nor do we have any clear idea about the political program Young is advocating. It is not enough to argue for new forms of knowledge and pedagogy. We need to know *what* forms and *which* pedagogy. Presumably, part of the new forms of knowledge would include knowledge about capitalist society but this Young, at present, does not provide. Since radical *practice* presupposes radical *theory*, we have a right to ask of Young what is the content of his understandings? And through which organizational forms are the alliances to be forged with other radical groups? Some specification of possible class alliances is called for which necessitates a clear enunciation of the various fractions of the different classes and the social basis for their potential radicalization. Moreover, we need more than a vague outline of the issues around which some form of class unity can be achieved. It is not enough to call for the creation of the elements of a socialist future. An effective counter-hegemony would entail not simply a thorough-going, theoretical critique of all facets of capitalism but also the articulation of a political program that can both bring about political unity among the various anti-capitalist sections and produce a crisis of hegemony. As yet, Young's commitment has not led him to specify clearly enough the nature of his program beyond mere voluntaristic appeals to action. A sounder theory of education, and of political practice within it, requires a more sustained attempt both to understand the nature of capitalist society and the various class forces within it. It presupposes a much more concerted attempt to come to grips with the nature of capitalism as a mode of production and its varying articulations in different social formations, using the 'comparative and historical framework' which Young argued for in 1971. Above all it requires a theory of ideology. The latter is necessary because it is quite clear that ideology is not only a set of ideas which sustain social inequality but a material level of social practice which is to a great extent unconscious. A political program which does not recognize the unconscious elements of ideology and its embodiment in social routines and rituals at all levels of social existence, and which relies simply on cultural critiques at the level of ideas, is doomed to failure. So is a political practice which does not locate the state as the crucial moment of class power and *the* significant object of a radical, socialist, political practice.

Conclusion

The argument in this chapter has centred on the lack of a theory of the capitalist mode of production and the role of ideology in its reproduction. It is now time to spell out more explicitly the Marxist theory of ideology before proceeding to show how its insights can illuminate the forms and processes of schooling in capitalist societies.

4 The theory of ideology

The theory of ideology in Marx and Engels

The work of Marx and Engels provides a series of brilliant insights into the socio historic genesis of ideas and their role in history generally, as well as the basis for a powerful analysis and critique of ideology in capitalist societies specifically. However, their theory is not without problems and lacunae. It developed through a series of transformations and the final and most fruitful formulation, as set out in the theory of commodity fetishism, was never expounded as rigorously or systematically as that pertaining to the economic instance of capitalist social formations. It has nevertheless been of enormous significance for the analysis of art, literature and other cultural forms and for the understanding of the role of law and of political and related processes, and, it will be argued here, is the single most important, though neglected, set of ideas for developing a sophisticated understanding of the role of education in capitalist societies.

Marx's materialist theory of history is set out in its most terse and pregnant form in the Preface to *A Contribution to the Critique of Political Economy* (Marx, 1970):

> In the social production of their existence, men inevitably enter into definite relations which are independent of their will, namely relations of production appropriate to a given state of development of their material forces of production. The totality of these relations of production constitutes the economic structure of society, the real foundation, on which arises a legal and political superstructure and to which correspond definite forms of social consciousness. The mode of production of material life conditions the general process of social political and intellectual life. It is not the consciousness of men that determines their existence, but their social existence that determines their consciousness.

At a certain stage of development the material productive forces of society come into conflict with the existing relations of production or – this merely expresses the same thing in legal terms – with the property relations within the framework of which they have operated hereto. From forms of development of the productive forces these relations turn into their fetters. Then begins an era of social revolution. The changes in the economic foundation lead sooner or later to the transformation of the whole immense superstructure. In studying such transformations it is always necessary to distinguish between the material transformation of the economic conditions of production, which can be determined with the precision of natural science, and the legal, political, religious, artistic or philosophic – in short, ideological forms, in which men become conscious of this conflict and fight it out. (1970, pp. 20–1)

Despite ambiguities, Marx is clear in this passage on a number of points: that it is not what he has referred to earlier as the 'general development of the human mind' which is the dynamic force in history, but the dialectic between the forces and relations of production; and that the mode of production of material life is the key category for understanding the genesis of political, legal and other ideological forms and their transformation. As he states elsewhere:

We must begin by stating the first premise of all human existence and therefore of all history, the premise namely that men must be in a position to live in order to be able to make history. But life involves before everything else eating and drinking, housing, clothing and various other things. The first historical act is thus the production of the means to satisfy these needs, the production of material life itself. (Marx, 1976)

Finally, and not the least importantly, the passage stresses like so many others, that the analysis of historic change has to go beyond the prevailing forms of social consciousness through which the world is understood:

Whilst in ordinary life every shopkeeper is very well able to distinguish between what someone professes to be and what he really is, our historiography has not yet won this trivial insight. It takes every epoch at its word and believes that everything it says and imagines about itself is true. (1976, p. 62)

Nevertheless the ambiguities in the Preface to the *Critique* remain. Many have cited it as evidence that Marx's theory of history is basically technologically determinist. Moreover, it seems to suggest that ideas are mechanically determined by the base and have no independent existence or causal efficacy, that they are merely epiphenomena. On this point, Engels was at pains to correct what he saw as serious distortions of his own and Marx's work:

> According to the materialist conception of history the ultimately determining element in history is the production and reproduction of real life. More than this, neither Marx nor I have ever asserted. Hence, if someone twists this into saying that the economic element is the only determining one, he transforms that proposition into a meaningless abstract senseless phrase. The economic situation is the basis but the various elements of the superstructure – political forms, . . . juridical forms . . . theories . . . also exercise their influence upon the course of the historical struggles and in many cases preponderate in determining their form. There is an interaction of all these elements in which . . . the economic movement finally asserts itself as necessary. (Engels, 1890, p. 498)

However, this attempt at clarification leaves almost as many problems open as it resolves, especially the question of the ultimate determinacy of the economic. Marxists, especially those influenced by Althusser, have often engaged in verbal games to avoid possible charges of economic reductionism whilst still adhering to a notion of the explanatory primacy of 'the economic'. Some of the confusion is due to the narrowness within which the concept of the economic is often defined. In Marx's work the economic is a far broader concept than in bourgeois social theory. It includes ideas, knowledge and social relationships. The idea of the determinacy of the economic can best be explained by referring to the way in which Marxists periodize human history in terms, as we have seen, of different modes of production. The latter are distinguished from each other in the first instance (Banaji, 1977) according to differing modes of extracting surplus labour from the direct producers. Feudalism is thus to be distinguished from capitalism by virtue of the role which extra-economic coercion plays, via religion and the state, in the appropriation of surplus labour; under capitalism appropriation occurs via the wage relation and takes the form of surplus value. The idea of the determinacy of the economic suggests that the political and ideological requirements for sustaining a specific mode of appropriating surplus labour can vary only within certain limits. As Williams puts it, (1973) new social relations and new kinds of social practice may be imagined but cannot be achieved unless the determining limits of a particular mode of production have been surpassed in practice by actual social change. For example, the full realization of the genuinely radical demands in the worker participation movement in capitalist societies today would presuppose the abolition of the wage relation as the mode of appropriating surplus labour and therefore of the capital relation generally.

Engels, warnings against a crude mechanistic determinism unfortunately went largely unheeded for more than half a century. By the time of the Second International, much Marxist thinking on ideology and politics was framed within a naive dualist approach where the complexities of the interrelationship between social phenomena were resolved through a mechanical reductionism or economism. The worst excesses of this approach are exemplified in the later writings of Kautsky, in Bernstein and in the official Stalinist orthodoxy. But neither Engels nor Marx himself are entirely free from responsibility for the direction in which Marxism in its theoretical moment moved, especially in its treatment of the problem of ideology. In *The German Ideology*, for example, there are a number of formulations which lend support to a reductivist approach to ideology, and although this work was not published until long after its authors died, similar formulations found their way into many other examples of their thinking, even into *Capital* where a far more complex and productive view of ideology was in the early stages of elaboration.

In *The German Ideology* and the *Theses on Feuerbach* (1845) Marx and Engels' earlier essentialist view of man gives way to one which emphasizes that men can be understood only as products of social relations – inside, not outside, history. However, the social formation, the ensemble of these social relations, is viewed as an expressive totality where the elements of the superstructure are all subject to some inner principle of development which emanates from the economic base. Ideas and other aspects of consciousness are thought of and described as merely 'reflexes' or 'echoes' of more real social processes, and are thereby reduced to epiphenomenal forms which have no reality of their own. An image which Marx and Engels use to describe this relationship is that of a 'camera obscura':

If in all ideology men and their circumstances appear upside-
down as in a camera obscura, this phenomenon arises just as
much from their historical life-process as the inversion of objects
on the retina does from their physical life processes. . . . We
set out from real active men, and on the basis of their real
life process we demonstrate the development of the reflexes and
echoes of this life process. The phantoms formed in the human
brain are also, necessarily, sublimates of their material life
process which is empirically verifiable and bound to material
premises (1976, p. 36)

There are also in *The German Ideology* frequent references to the
notion of ideology as false consciousness. We do not wish to reject
entirely a concept of false consciousness, for reasons which will be
elaborated below, but the formulation here is inadequate. Those who
think ideologically are conceived as having misrecognized or misper-
ceived true reality, their ideological conceptions being merely false or
distorted representations of it. Such a concept of false consciousness
which treats ideological notions as referring to nothing in reality at
all is misleading. Moreover, ruling ideas are referred to in *The German
Ideology* as those of the dominant class by virtue of its control over
the means of ideological dissemination – the press, schools, churches
and so on. This sometimes leads to a conceptualization of subordinate
classes as passively manipulated victims of propaganda disseminated by
a cynical and self-interested, but all-knowing ruling class; it thus reinforces a naive conspiracy theory of society, and tends to reduce the
concept of ideology to nothing but lies.

The ideas of the ruling class are in every epoch the ruling ideas;
i.e., the class which is the ruling material force of society is at the
same time its ruling intellectual force . . . so that the ideas of those
who lack the means of mental production are on the whole subject
to it. . . . The ruling ideas are nothing more than the ideal expression
of dominant material relations. . . . The ruling class individuals
composing the ruling class possess among other things consciousness
and therefore think. . . . (pp. 59–60)

The same passage later refers to thinkers of the ruling class as 'its active
conceptive ideologists who make the formation of the illusions of the
class about itself its chief source of livelihood.'

Despite these criticisms, there remain some vital ideas in *The German
Ideology* which reappear in Marx's more mature work. Among the

most vital is the rejection of a view of social change as being dependent upon prior changes in consciousness:

> This conception of history has not . . . like the idealist view of history to look for a category in every period but remains constantly on the real ground of history; it does not explain practice from the idea, but explains the formation of ideas from material practice, and accordingly it comes to the conclusion that all forms and products of consciousness cannot be dissolved by mental criticism . . . but only by the practical overthrow of the actual social relations which give rise to this idealist humbug. (pp. 53–4)

Although some of the more unfortunate language and imagery of *The German Ideology* persists in *Capital*, this later work offers an outline of a far more sophisticated and adequate theory: that of commodity fetishism (Marx, 1974a). Marx has now moved beyond the view of society as an expressive totality to the notion of a mode of production characterized by different, relatively autonomous levels – the political, the ideological, and the economic – which are articulated with each other but are not mutually reducible (Althusser and Balibar, 1970). Instead of ideas being seen as mere epiphenomena, which spring from the real economic relations, they are characterized as apprehensions of real 'phenomenal forms' or 'appearances', of real underlying relations. They are no longer seen as false in the sense of *illusory*, because they *do* refer to something in reality, albeit something refracted and transfigured in consciousness.

Ideologies are seen as systems of representations which signify a set of relationships which are real but which hide another set of relations between people which are no less real. They are not seen as merely 'disguised metaphors of class relations', but as having a reality of their own, an internal patterning, *sui generis*. They do produce inversions and distortions, but it is precisely because, so to speak, they gear into real social practices and routines, that they are so hard to transform. This point will be elaborated below when the notion of practical ideologies is discussed. Suffice it to say here that the theory of commodity fetishism provides the starting point for a concept of ideology as a system of representations or significations. As Hall has argued, quoting Bourdieu, we need to be able to understand the way in which

> the field of ideological positions reproduces the field of social positions in a transfigured form and be able to account for the

mechanisms which consistently sustain in reality a set of representations which are not so much false to, as false inflections of, the real relations on which they in fact depend.

(Hall, 1977b)

The world of appearances, what appears on the surface, does have a reality and that reality is absolutely necessary for capitalist production. As Mepham argues, 'it is not the bourgeois class which is the source of ideology, but bourgeois society itself' (Mepham, 1973). The insertion of the subject into capitalist relations of production (of which Marx himself does not provide an account) involves also inserting him into the 'phenomenal forms' of capitalist production. This idea will become clearer when the concept of the subject and of ideology as material practices is considered below.

Marx himself made no distinction between theoretical ideology and practical ideologies and, indeed, seems to make the former the model of what he means by ideology proper; nor did he provide any specifically materialist theory of the human subject, i.e. generate a psychology founded upon his view of the systematic structuring of social reality, via the material productive process (Jacka, 1977). Both these issues, however, have been taken up by contemporary Marxists. The major weakness of Marx's account, and indeed of later theories concerning ideology, is the lack of any adequate appraisal of how those who live their lives *within* ideology can be brought to transcend it. No satisfactory theory of the route to true knowledge has been offered. The political importance of this question is self-evident but its solution is not. Some tentative suggestions will be made at the end of this chapter.

Before discussing the post-Marx developments in the Marxist theory of ideology, it is necessary to make some comments on that non-Marxist tradition in the study of ideas which is often referred to as the sociology of knowledge. It is important to differentiate a Marxist account of ideology from its bourgeois counterparts, especially in a work on education, since it is the latter rather than the Marxists who have dominated the development of the discipline. This is so not because of any sinister conspiracy against what Marxists might have to say about education, but because, until very recently, Marxists have had exceedingly little to say about it of any interest. In Chapters 1 and 2 an attempt was made to give a materialist account of changes in social thought about education. The past silences of Marxism concerning these issues need to be understood within this framework.

Marxism and the sociology of knowledge

In common with classical Marxist theory, the sociology of knowledge has tended to confine itself to the analysis of high-level, systematized bodies of ideological theories articulated by those groups whom we might think of as the socially defined intelligentsia. The division between mental and manual labour which Marx saw was so important for class formation has not been seen as producing any fundamental discontinuity between the full-time ideologues of a society and the ordinary members of the classes whose interests they are said to articulate. The common assumption in both Marxism and the sociology of knowledge seems to be that social practices and relations in ordinary life are in some crucial sense structured and mediated by such high-level theories. Until writers like Schutz, few had bothered to explore the practical consciousness of everyday life, even though it should be self-evident that common-sense man is often very different from those who live by and through their ideas, in that he literally has more *common* sense.

Although the sociology of knowledge and Marxism share this defect, there is a fundamental opposition between them in terms of methodology and problematic. Though Marx has hovered as an absent presence over the sociology of knowledge, as was seen in Chapter 2, its main problematic has been an attempt to refute him. The account of ideology in terms of a theory of the internal structures and dynamics of social formations, the primacy of the concept of mode of production, the necessity for a class analysis of the historical genesis of ideas and their social function, is not accepted as the prime methodological and theoretical premise. Even when the class basis of ideas is treated as a fruitful, albeit one-sided, hypothesis, there is a failure to explore the analysis within some conception of a socio-historic totality which ontologically consists of something more than pure ideas. Indeed, with some notable exceptions, the categories utilized in the sociology of knowledge tend to be descriptivist, empiricist and ahistorical. The whole discipline has tended to lack theoretical rigour (Jacka, 1977).

Another major difference between the two approaches is the tendency towards an idealist solution to the subject/object dualism within which the problem of the role of ideas in history tends to be thought. In good Kantian tradition, it is ultimately the individual knowing subject who makes and remakes his phenomenal world. Indeed, in both the Durkheimian strand, via structural-functionalism and ethnomethodology, and in the German idealist strand via Dilthey, Simmel, Mead and social phenomenology, there is a strong predisposition to reduce social reality to the realm of ideas. In addition to this philosophical idealism, there is a strong push towards epistemological relativism. Since the individual constitutes his world, how can different accounts of that world be arbitrated? Given that extra-ideal factors intrude into the world of 'pure' (yet impure) theory, and given the absence of Mannheim's socially unattached intellectuals, they cannot be; there are no epistemologically privileged criteria by which to judge between truth and falsity, except presumably those that assert that all knowledge is relative. This tendency to relativism and scepticism in the sociology of knowledge is undoubtedly linked with the tradition of philosophical idealism which has often been characterized by Marxists as the philosophical self-consciousness of the bourgeoisie.

Finally, the sociology of knowledge lacks any explicit political commitment, let alone a revolutionary commitment to overcome the limitations of class society or adherence to Marx's dictum that the point is not to understand the world but to change it. This is not to assert, of course, that it lacks an implicit theoretical commitment. It is hardly an exaggeration to say that all its chief classical exponents, those we discussed in Chapter 2, have been in some strong sense ideologues of capitalism. Whilst they may have been vocal in what they saw as the defects of contemporary societies, the limits of their thinking were constrained by a bourgeois world view, a view which does not, and cannot, comprehend that the capital relation itself has to be transcended.

Practical ideologies and their material embodiment

In contemporary Marxism, the concept of ideology refers not merely to abstract systems of thought, institutionally recognized as such – for example liberalism, as articulated by Locke, Bentham or Mill, or conservatism by Burke or Michael Oakeshott – but to something much broader. Althusser writes of ideology as being the way individuals live their relation to their real conditions of existence, invoking a sense of ideology as lived experience rather than merely thought (Althusser, 1971b). Abstract theoretical systems will be called here 'theoretical ideologies', as distinct from what Althusser terms 'practical ideologies' and Volosinov (discussed below) 'behavioural ideologies' (Volosinov, 1973). There is obviously an ongoing dialectical relationship between the two levels of ideology which cannot be discussed in any detail here, but most contemporary writers in the Marxist tradition would

95

argue that the latter is both historically and analytically prior. Althusser defined practical ideologies thus:

> Practical ideologies are complex formations of montages [sets] of notions – representations – images, on the one hand and of montages [sets] of behaviour – conduct – attitudes and gestures on the other. The whole functions as the practical norms which govern the attitude and the taking up of concrete positions by men with respect to the real objects and the real problems of their social and individual existence and of their history.
> (quoted in Heath, 1972)

In short, the concept of practical ideologies invokes a socially defined way of thinking and acting, a set of conventions and assumptions which make meaning possible and which phenomenologists call the taken-for-granted world of everyday life. It is thus somewhat akin to what sociologists refer to as culture. However, unlike the phenomenologists' concept of the 'taken-for-granted', normative institutions which determine 'what everyone does' and 'what everyone knows', practical ideologies, in the Marxist sense, are seen as not merely cultural but having a material reality and a material force. For example, every phenomena which functions as an ideological sign has some kind of material embodiment. The everyday objects which surround us are often infused with ideological meaning, as advertisers and media managers know only too well. Most importantly, practical ideologies are embedded in concrete patterned behaviours which have more than just cultural or conceptual significance.

Practical ideologies and production relations

A Marxist account of practical ideologies would necessarily involve their location within an analysis of production relations, not in the sense that the latter mechanistically determine the former, but in the sense of their inseparability. By this is meant that practical ideologies both develop within and are a necessary element of definite social relations of production. The Marxist concept of production relations cannot be understood, however, unless both its aspects are grasped. On the one hand, man has a relationship to nature and the instruments of production – a technical aspect; on the other he has a social relationship with other people, for example with those who own the means of production – machinery, factories, raw materials, etc. – or with the direct producers (Clarke, 1977). With respect to both aspects, consciousness enters in. Practical ideologies are a necessary element of the material social process. Men producing have ideas and habits referring to nature and tools, for example, or concepts of social relationships within the labour process, or socio-political notions and rituals regarding the context of production itself. The bourgeois concept of production is much narrower and refers merely to the man-nature relationship in its technical aspect. The resulting confusion about the meaning of the concept has been a source of much unnecessary argument and scepticism regarding the thesis of the explanatory priority of the mode of production in history. In a Marxist account the conditions of ideological reproduction of the social formation are to be found in production itself and not merely externally. In the ongoing routines of the labour process, through the habit of submission to authority, for example, practical ideologies are reproduced and reinforced.

Language and ideology

In the last decade, much of the advances made in the understanding of ideology has centred on the question of language. Since social and cultural phenomena are infused with semiotic meaning and ideology has been defined as a sign system, linguistics, as the study of verbal signs and the most theoretically advanced branch of semiology (the study of systems of signs) has been explored as a theoretically fruitful source of insights into the workings of ideology. Without wishing to discuss the more esoteric and often pretentious debates regarding structural linguistics and its compatibility with a materialist account of society and history, the significance of language as a central concern in the study of ideology must not be underestimated. Words are basic to any sort of communication. Language enables things to mean and is the mediator of ideological signs. Whilst not wishing to go as far as Wittgenstein 'It is not experience that organizes expression but the other way round. ... The limits of my language mean the limits of my world', it is clear that all experience is subject to at least the partial press of language.

What is so important about language? Language is a coding system which classifies and organizes the external objective world in some kind of meaningful way. Words are not merely names for things 'out there', standing in a one to one relationship with them, as a nominalist might think, but derive their meaning from their embeddedness within a whole structure of language – and, some would argue, from their non-linguistic context as well. And it is this *structure* of language as a coding system which articulates and defines how events, phenomena and people are to be interpreted. Ideology cannot be reduced to, nor thought of as identical with language, but the way in which men come to understand their world and act within it is subject to the mediation of language. Hence its importance. Language and thought both partially presuppose the other. Language is not a mere tool for communicating thoughts, since what has to be communicated is already, at least partially, subject to the encoding potential of language.

There are two main strands of linguistics which have contributed to the Marxist analysis of ideology. The older and more influential, at least in French Marxism, has been that based on the work of Ferdinand de Saussure (1974). It has influenced structural anthropology, in the work of Lévi-Strauss in particular (1966, 1973), semiotics in writers like Barthes (1967, 1972) and the contributors to journals such as *Screen*, structuralist Marxism in Althusser and Poulantzas, and Lacanian psychoanalysis. The other less well known but potentially more productive strand emanates from the work of Volosinov (1973), a Russian linguist and Marxist writing in the 1920s until disposed of by Stalin (who, interestingly, considered himself something of an expert on the question of where one locates language in the base/superstructure model). Volosinov's work has only recently been translated and discussed, but his contribution lies firmly within a historical materialist problematic and already has been the subject of some exciting developments in the empirical study of ideologies – for example at the Centre for Cultural Studies in Birmingham (Woolfson, 1976; Tolson, 1976).

Saussure was not himself a Marxist. On the contrary, his work can be viewed as fitting comfortably within that idealist, anti-Marxist tradition which as we have seen pervaded European intellectual life in the first two decades of the twentieth century (Hughes, 1959). Linguistics for Saussure was the study of the underlying structure of languages in general and perhaps the discovery of general rules of language as such. He made a clear distinction between what he called *language* (the system of language) and *parole* (the individual realizations of that system – or concrete speech utterances, as Volosinov, whom we discuss below, defined them). Saussure argued that the proper object of study for linguistics was the former, the abstract formal analysis of the hidden structure of language as a relational system of words. Another important distinction he made was between the synchronic and diachronic study of language. Since linguistic change was, he argued, fortuitous, individual, arbitrary and lacking in any structure, the synchronic was the only proper field of enquiry – i.e., one should study language at any one point in time and elucidate its inner structure.

It is unnecessary here to give any detailed account or assessment of his work. Suffice it to say that in terms of the study of ideology his emphasis on the unconscious structure of language – that those who speak language do not 'know' it (we know not whereof we speak . . .) – is of great importance and has assisted the further clarification of the notion of ideology as being at least partly unconscious. His emphasis on words being systematically related to each other, these relationships giving individual words their meaning is likewise important. It helps us to see the need for building a view of ideology as involving, not a whole series of isolated unrelated fragments, but a coherent and systematic patterning of its elements. Furthermore, the inference that one can draw from his work, that there is a real sense in which the structure of our language may, in fact, constrain thought – that it is not we who think and then use words but our language that thinks for us – all of this is of seminal import for any account of ideology and its power.

The legacy is not, however, altogether on the positive side. In Lévi-Strauss, for example, there is a tendency to detach the study of signs – language and other cultural coding systems – from any extra linguistic reality, in spite of the crucial role of context for meaning (Timpanaro, 1975). Indeed, there is a tendency in some of those influenced by Saussure to reduce the social to nothing but the semiotic. Similarly, Althusser's attempt to build a regional theory of the ideological level, whilst asserting the importance of its articulation with the other levels, is not successful. Of greater concern, however, is the ahistorical static framework of analysis which fails to capture a significant aspect of all languages, namely, their constant transformation in the course of being spoken and the arbitrariness of fixing languages at any particular point in time for the purpose of discovering their hidden structure. By neglecting the diachronic, and by refusing to look at concrete language utterances in context, Saussure (and Lévi-Strauss) seem to locate the source of any structure and unity in language outside the historical process in some deep-level cultural universals with their roots possibly in some essentialist nature of the human mind. Such a thesis, which is not demonstrable, conflicts with one of the most basic tenets of historical materialism, namely the social production of man's being in history and the rejection of any essentialist anthropology. Moreover, the conservative political implications of a view of conscious thought and expression, as well as the rules defining social relationships, being limited and constrained by some pre-symbolic, pre-social function, are akin to those emanating from social theories which explain social inequalities as being due to natural differences between people, as, in some way, the result of human nature.

Volosinov's work (1973) is more productive of a materialist view of language, as well as of a Marxist social and cognitive psychology which, he argues, should be grounded in a theory of ideology. 'Individual consciousness is not the architect of the ideological superstructure' he writes, 'but only a tenant lodging in the social edifice of ideological signs.' He offers what is still an important and pertinent critique of Saussure's work for its idealism, ahistoricism, essentialism, and its neglect of parole – or verbal utterances – which he wants to locate as the central object of a materialist account of language. Moreover, language use should, in his view, be studied in its social and historical context. The basic social category for understanding variations and difference in speech forms and themes is that of class or production relations: 'Production relations and the socio-political order shaped by those relations determine the full range of verbal contacts between people, all the forms and means of their verbal communication at work, in political life, in ideological creativity' (p. 19). The key to understanding ideology is thus language, and the unit of study for linguistics is the word. 'The word is the ideological phenomenon *par excellence*' (p. 13). Words in themselves, are neutral, but they become partisan because of their central position within ideologies viewed as signifying practices. Three methodological prescriptions for the analysis of language and ideology are offered: that it should not be divorced from the material reality of signs; the sign should not be divorced from the concrete forms of social intercourse; and that communication and its forms need to be related to the material base. The emphasis on the context is fruitful because a consideration of the fundamental social relationships between speakers and hearers is an essential prerequisite for any imputation of meaning. Words themselves have no intrinsic meaning but are given meaning and content by their structured location within behavioural ideologies.

Volosinov advocates a historical analysis of what he terms the inner dialectical movement of the sign, i.e., the variation in word meanings between social groups. Signs become an arena of the class struggle: 'Existence is not merely reflected in signs but refracted by an intersecting of differently oriented social interests within one and the same sign community, i.e., by the class struggle.' The inner dialectical quality of the sign comes out only in times of social crisis, when there is a breakdown of hegemony (see below). This is because in 'normal' times, whilst there is considerable variation in word accenting or the imputation of meanings to words, given the different social relations of production, linguistic communication is subject to the relations of dominance in the society – not all have equal power to define reality, linguistically, for others. Nevertheless, just taking the example of the word 'liberty', it is obvious to anyone who has studied a little history that what this word means and has meant in different historical periods and for different groups has varied enormously. Raymond Williams's book *Keywords* (1976) provides many excellent other examples. Similarly, the history of anti-colonial movements offers many illustrations of this point, the national bourgeoisie having often used the liberal rhetoric of terms like 'freedom' and 'equality' against the colonial rulers, only to have them turned against them later by participants in more radical social movements.

Volosinov's work also throws up exciting notions regarding the question of ruling-class hegemony and its relationship to patterns of linguistic dominance. He argues that ruling classes always strive to make verbal and other ideological signs uni-accented, or with a completely unambiguous meaning which serves their interests: Moreover:

> In the ordinary conditions of life, the contradictions embedded
> in every ideological sign cannot emerge fully because the
> ideological sign is an established dominant ideology. Dominant
> ideology is always somewhat reactionary and tries as it were, to
> stabilise the preceding factor in the dialectical flux of the
> social generative process, so accentuating yesterday's truth
> as to make is appear today's – and that is what is responsible
> for the refracting and distorting peculiarity of the ideological
> sign within the dominant ideology.

The concept of hegemony

So far, we have made little mention of the concept of a dominant ideology, but in a class society, the practical ideologies within which people live their everyday lives occur within specific relations of domination and subordination which are related to the distribution of

power. Thus everyday practical ideologies are structured, and intersected, by the forms and themes of dominant meanings and values.
It will be useful to discuss this in terms of Gramsci's concept of hegemony (Gramsci, 1971).

Gramsci was an Italian Marxist who fell victim to fascism, but
not before he had both had a significant effect on the organization
of a working-class movement in Italy and had made a profound contribution to the development of Marxist theory. He was the first to
expound systematically the concept of hegemony and identify its
political significance. Gramsci was interested in the differences in the
relationship between the state and civil society in Russia compared with
the more stable socio-democratic regimes of western Europe. In the
latter, he argued, the bourgeois class consolidates its rule through a
process of ideological hegemony, the mobilization of spontaneous
consent through the workings of the institutions of civil society – the
family, churches, the press, and schools. In Russia, by comparison,
the state's coercive role was both more necessary and more visible,
given the failure of the ruling class to acquire a hegemonic position
vis à vis other classes. Anderson, in a brilliant analysis of Gramsci's
work, has documented the ambiguity and shifting characterization of
the precise relationship between state and civil society, but fully endorses
the heuristic value of the concept, both theoretically and politically
(Anderson, 1977). Hegemony refers to a set of assumptions, theories,
practical activities, a world view through which the ruling class exerts
its dominance. Its function is to reproduce on the ideological plain the
conditions for class rule and the continuation of the social relations of
production. Hegemonic beliefs and practices thus shape practical
ideologies and penetrate the level of common sense, mixing and mingling
with ideological practices more spontaneously generated.

The concept of ideological hegemony does not mean that non-
dominant classes are ideologically manipulated through and through
in some over-determined way. On the contrary, Gramsci took pains
to stress that hegemony has to be fought for against countervailing
tendencies produced by the structural location of the working class in
the labour process and elsewhere; indeed, he emphasized the contradictory nature of common sense. Working-class men, for example,
often experience a fundamental discontinuity between the social
relations in which they are involved at work and those they encounter
within the family, the local community, the trade union and elsewhere.
Each of these different locales may give rise to varying and perhaps

competing tendencies in their practical ideology, the whole leading to a fundamental dissociation at the level of consciousness.

Common sense is, thus, never simply and purely the result of hegemony. It contains elements spontaneously generated, residual elements handed down intergenerationally (even though the conditions which produced them by now may have disappeared) and borrowings from inter-class contact, as well as being intersected and moulded by the operation of hegemony into some kind of contradictory unit. Moreover, common sense responds to changes in the socio-historical process. Hegemony has to be viewed, then, as a dynamic movement continually responding to unresolved conflicts and new ideological tendencies. Hegemonic practice succeeds when it has produced an unquestioned, taken-for-granted attitude towards how things are, when subjects identify themselves within limits defined by the hegemonic meanings and operate unconsciously, via their ideological practice, within premises which both derive from and help to reproduce the *status quo*. But this is the ruling-class ideal. In practice, new ideological initiatives are continually emerging both within and without the dominant hegemony. Nothing is ever static. Emergent ideological practices arise, some oppositional, some counter-hegemonic, some which are easily absorbed or incorporated, within the basic terms of the hegemonic form. Raymond Williams, in an incisive commentary on the base/superstructure model, has developed his earlier notion of a selective tradition at work within the dominant culture to analyse these dynamic aspects of hegemonic practice (Williams, 1973, 1977b). The selective tradition continually makes and remakes the dominant culture, in response to changing initiatives, in a manner which tries to safeguard the fundamental relations of production through a drive to incorporate and thereby transform any initiatives which threaten the capital relation and promise to weaken the bourgeois state. It is one of the functions of hegemony to isolate any such initiatives from the material social process, to recreate a fetishized separation of the class struggle from the political process – a function analogous to the role of the dominant ideology in fostering an illusion of the independence of education from politics.

It is not suggested that hegemonic practice is always successful; there is no assertion of a functionalist tendency for a stable equilibrium to be established via its normal activities. There is of course a tendency for dominant meanings to prevail, given the control by the hegemonic class over the means whereby practical ideologies are structured and moulded. This explains why even counter-hegemonic initiatives often tend to be framed in terms of the rhetoric and content of the dominant hegemonic form. Moreover, as Gramsci perceived, the very fact that many of the organizations of the working class develop out of what were once purely defensive institutions produces a situation where the terms within which opposition to the ruling class is articulated are such as to leave the main parameters of the *status quo* untouched. As Williams has so ably argued, the dominant culture even seems to control and produce its own counter-culture. Nevertheless, hegemony does sometimes break down in times of acute social crisis. In Russia, for example, the Revolution of 1917 occurred after the prevailing hegemony had been disrupted. Similarly, in Germany at the end of the Second World War, there was a severe collapse in social control which had problematic implications for the security of capitalist relations of production, a situation which the allied commanders took immediate steps to remedy in the occupation period, resorting, in many instances, to quite repressive measures. It is at those moments, when the state of hegemony is extremely precarious, that one can see clearly the indissolubility of force and consent, coercion and hegemony, in the maintenance of bourgeois class power.

At any one point in time, however, when there is no great threat to hegemony, dominant emergent and residual meanings co-exist within the structure of hegemony in a complex unity. It is for this reason that any attempt to define any close, one to one, relationship between the cultural superstructure and the economic base is difficult. The fact that history is always on the move should not be neglected.

The discussion in the previous chapter has stressed continually the role of the state in any account of the ongoing process of hegemony. Some writers neglect the important question of political power and the coercive apparatus of the state, consensual order and stability becoming merely a question of the cultural dominance of the ruling class. Representatives of the Frankfurt school have often been criticized for doing this. But to demonstrate the experiential force of hegemony is not the same as proving its structural primacy (Eagleton, 1976).

In Marxist social theory, the state is thought of as the sphere where the organization of class power takes place through the co-ordination of the different class fractions into a power bloc (Poulantzas, 1975b). The state operates, among other things, to shape and produce a consensus through the selective forms of social knowledge made available and the moulding of ideological practice. However, the state's role in hegemony is not merely concerned with the question of ideological domination but with the maintenance of spontaneous consent through the granting of economic concessions and through political organization. The end of state practice in capitalist class society is the guaranteeing of the conditions for continual capital accumulation, the maintenance of capitalist relations of production, the insertion of agents into their respective positions within the social formation. Depending on the socio-historic conditions, the interrelationship between force and consent will vary. But, as Anderson argues, even in stable conditions, when there is no attack on the prevailing hegemony, there is, simultaneously, at the centre of the social democratic state, the specific way in which the bourgeois class has preferred to exercise its rule, a silent absence (1977). The machinery for repression and violence hover here, and coercion thus provides the key explanatory category for understanding the success of bourgeois rule and its apparent legitimation through the operation of hegemony.

The constitution of the subject

If individuals live their lives within ideology as we have defined it, then the role of the individual in history is rendered problematic. Some are reluctant to accept any thesis which gives theoretical primacy to the social and undervalues the role of consciousness and individual freedom in shaping the course of history. Yet it is important to query what is meant by the notion of the individual – merely the biological organism, with a definite physical make-up and potential, or does the concept include some reference to the individual's ideas, aspirations, abilities, freedom, moral dispositions and other cultural attributes? If the latter, then our concept is of an individual already social, the product of society and history, not *qua* animal, a pre-social, merely biological being. We should therefore eschew any arbitrary opposition between the individual on the one hand and society and history on the other.

Nevertheless, until recently, the problem of the individual has been inadequately theorized within a historical materialist framework. With Marx and Engels, for example, there is a tendency to oscillate between on the one hand a view of man as the passive victim of propaganda, manipulated through ruling-class control over the instruments for disseminating ideas, a victim of false consciousness but ultimately achieving true consciousness by the inexorable workings

105

of the infrastructural contradictions; and on the other hand, a view of man as engaged in an ongoing dialectic to overcome self-alienation and objectification to recover a true human essence. The former view, as we have argued, leads to a mechanistic approach to the relationship between ideas and the 'base' and provides no entrée into the problem of subjectivity; the latter, through its commitment to the notion of a human essence, cannot grasp the historical specificity of the forms of human consciousness and subjectivity, and reproduces, in ideological form, the notion of primacy of the individual subject's consciousness in history.

In recent years this theoretical inadequacy has been recognized. It is seen to be a problem not merely of rejecting bourgeois psychologies of the individual which tend to reinforce the artificial separation of the individual and society, but of attempting a theory which will account for the processes and mechanisms whereby the subject, of which bourgeois theory speaks, is produced within the social formation; a subject having a concept of his/her own essence, with thoughts, emotions, purposes, who categorizes himself and the world, and who sees his own essence as the source of his activity and projects and as the centre of his symbolic universe. Such a theory owes much to the contributions of structural anthropology (via Lévi-Strauss), structural linguistics (via Saussure), semiotics (via Barthes and Kristeva, 1976) and psychoanalysis (via Freud and Lacan) (Lacan, 1968, 1970; Althusser, 1971a). None of these traditions of thought escape idealism and it should be noticed that their utilization by Marxists has not been without controversy or criticism. Nevertheless, some important ideas have been produced which help to conceptualize more adequately the relationship between ideology as social practice and individual consciousness.

In line with the rejection of methodological individualism, human consciousness is analysed within the framework, and from the perspective, of ideology. Ideology is seen as a level of the social formation and not as the sum total of the workings of individual consciousnesses. Both human consciousness and the subjectivity of the individual are seen as the effect, rather than the source, of ideology. The ideological is identified as a system of signifying practices, an elaborate texture of signs which give meaning and provide the trellis-work within which a symbolic order is produced and maintained (Adlam *et al.*, 1977). Human individuals become subjects by being inserted, to use Althusser's rather unsatisfactory phrase, into this symbolic universe of ideological meanings which pre-exist them. The process of insertion into these ideological meanings or signifying practices is one whereby the subjects' relation to meaning within the total available or potential universe of meanings is produced – i.e. subjectivity depends upon a social location within the ideological space of the social formation.

It may be misleading to speak of ideological meanings when referring to the constitution of the subject by insertion into these practices because such a term implies a degree of self-consciousness while living within ideology. Utilizing Freud's notion of the unconscious, recent contributions by Marxists to the theory of ideology have argued that the mechanisms which constitute the subject in ideology also create an unconscious (Coward and Ellis, 1977). Indeed the production of the unconscious may be the precondition for creating any sort of subjectivity at all. It is argued that much of what is meant by ideology is in fact unconscious, which explains the resistance of ideology to conscious reasoning and demonstrations of internal inconsistencies, etc., and throws light on why people do not always act in ways which seem to accord with their objective interests.

The 'rediscovery of the unconscious', of 'what is refused entry to consciousness' (Lacan), by Marxists is of great theoretical and political significance. It gives rise to an attempt to understand the dynamics of psychic life and the significance of unconscious processes for conscious existence. Lacan and others have argued that the unconscious is structured like a language and that its dynamics are due to the processes of signification and representation having implications for the conscious dimension of psychic life but in ways which evade the self understanding of the subject. In their analysis, consciousness moves from its central position as the originator of all action, knowledge and will and a concern develops for the mechanisms whereby the constituting yet partly unconscious subject develops.

In spite of the obvious ethnocentrism of many of Freud's views, the tendency towards a mechanistic approach which sometimes takes over from the linguistic analogy, and the lack of any adequate historical dimension to his analysis of psychic structures, his theory of the unconscious can, perhaps, offer some understanding of the forms and mechanisms of psychic life which are of use for building a more general theory regarding the constitution of the subject which transcends any particular historical conjuncture. Some, like Lacan and Kristeva, are convinced of its generalizability across different historical forms. Others argue that such a view involves another form of essentialism.

Why should the unconscious as Freud understood it not be merely a historically specific form of the unconscious which is not universal? Why should not subjects be as they appear on the surface when socialist relations of production prevail? Marx seemed to think that when things *are* as they *appear* there will be no need for social science, implying that it will be possible to see things as they really are, not through the medium of unconscious ideological spectacles.

The subject in bourgeois society

Whilst a comprehensive theory of ideology must be able to account for the different forms which individuality takes in different modes of production, this cannot be the concern here. This discussion will be limited to an analysis of the specific form of subjectivity in bourgeois society. The understanding of the ideological matrix within which the subject is produced in bourgeois society involves examining the forms of self-representation through the rituals and practices and myths which pervade every day existence, as well as through its more systematic and coherent articulation, to be found, for example, in bourgeois social and political theory.

In line with the theory of ideology outlined above, it should be emphasized that the forms of bourgeois subjectivity are not fixed and unchanging for all time. On the contrary, they are tied into the structure of hegemony which, as can be argued, has to be seen as an ever moving state of dominance over feelings and ideas which respond dynamically to the fluctuating balance of class forces. For example, as Macpherson shows, present-day bourgeois theory which underpins the ideological matrix of the social formation has developed out of a subtle accommodation to egalitarian and democratic beliefs and practices by the hegemonic ruling class (Macpherson, 1973). He shows how the characteristic features of the bourgeois subject are related historically to the rise of the bourgeois class in the seventeenth and eighteenth centuries and the generalization of market relations of exchange. Through a careful examination of the writings of Hobbes, Locke, the Levellers, etc., he draws out a portrait of the bourgeois subject, not explicitly discussed in their work but taken for granted and presupposed. He is the embodiment of possessive individualism, having proprietorship over his own person and abilities, free to alienate his own property and his capacity to labour, free from dependence on the will of others, voluntarily entering into contracts in accordance with his own calculation of his self-interest; capable of infinitely appropriating. Bourgeois man sees social relations as primarily market relations (Macpherson, 1961).

Political society is viewed as a necessary evil, a human contrivance for the protection of the individual's property in his person and his goods, a guarantee therefore for the maintenance of orderly relations of exchange. Each person is free, that is what makes him human, such freedom only permissibly being limited by such rules as protect the freedom of others (Macpherson, 1962).

The eighteenth-century bourgeois subject was thus the carrier of liberalism, a historically progressive ideology necessary for the rise of the bourgeois class and its struggle against the obstacles of feudal relations of production and the restrictions they entailed on capital and labour. But liberalism did not remain unchanged. In the class struggles of the French Revolution and the first half of the nineteenth century, it received a powerful challenge from a radical egalitarianism and democratic ideology. Modern liberal democratic theory is the result of a successful incorporation by liberalism of egalitarian notions which presented a radical challenge to its hegemony. The ideology and forms of parliamentary democracy are the result of this ongoing process of accommodation and incorporation which is characteristic of any hegemonic ideology.

Liberal democratic ideology, then, is the context, today, within which the bourgeois subject is constituted. What was once a historically specific set of ideas, by no means general, with a distinctive class basis, comes to be seen as natural, unchanging and unchangeable ('that's how things are'). The power relations which are peculiar to market society are seen as how things have always been and ought to be. They acquire a timelessness which is powerfully legitimized by a theory of human nature. Characteristic relationships of ownership, historically peculiar to market society and commodity exchange are read back into the nature of the individual such that the possibility of change becomes discounted and the social order is seen as a natural one. ('It's all to do with human nature.') Political struggles to alter present-day social arrangements are seen as futile for 'things are as they are' because of man's basic human attributes and nothing could ever be very different.

These pervasive representations of man and society are not merely abstractly stored in the head but are materialized in social practices and rituals which have explanatory priority. Few in present day society would be aware of the inner connection between their view of man, politics and society and its antecedents in the historical emergence of the bourgeois class. In addition, because these assumptions are embodied in and correspond with actual practices in everyday life, they are difficult to transcend until a society of market relations – i.e., a bourgeois society – has itself been transcended.

For example, the everyday operation of the market, the exchange of goods and services for money, in the rituals and practices which surround the wage relation, the payment for work done by the labourers, the freedom to enter into wage contracts, the very institution of the contract itself with its taken-for-granted equality between the contracting parties, all serve to diffuse commodity fetishism and reaffirm a belief in the fundamental freedom and equality in the market place, the root of individualism and the linchpin of bourgeois ideology. In the same way, the forms of the parliamentary state – its regular elections, its 'balance of power' through the apparent separation of the legislature, executive and the judiciary, the apparently democratic representation brought about by the party system, the seeming independence of the courts – all serve to reinforce notions of the independence of the state from the rest of civil society, its embodiment of the general will and its ability to safeguard the 'national interest'. Anderson calls the bourgeois democratic state the nub of the ideological apparatus (1977). This, together with the atomization caused by the organization of the labour process and the social relations of work with its hierarchies and advanced division of labour, serves to reproduce the ideological foundations of bourgeois social relations of production and reaffirm the symbolic representations of bourgeois society in the minds of the bourgeois subject.

Poulantzas has discussed the consequences of bourgeois ideology in terms of the production of what he calls a false unity, and an effect of isolation (Poulantzas, 1975b). By these terms he is referring to the way the bourgeois subject thinks in a fetishized way of the separation of politics from economics, conceiving of the state as somehow independent from civil society and above it, a neutral arbiter guaranteeing a sense of unity to the nation. Within ideology the social universe is divided into the public and the private; in the latter, autonomous free individuals enter into market exchanges with no common interests of a class character. Lacking any consciousness of themselves as members of classes, the dominated classes are demobilized whilst simultaneously the dominant classes or class fractions are organized to secure their class interests. Bourgeois ideology, whilst the product of class hegemony and helping to sustain it, is systematically silent regarding the existence of classes and the historical role they have played in the transition from one mode of production to another. History becomes the endless flux of events, historiography is concerned with the minutiae of exhaustively getting at the facts.

This process of depoliticization to which Poulantzas refers has been brilliantly explored by Barthes in the context of studies of the symbolism surrounding the themes of popular culture. In *Mythologies*, (1972) he traces a fundamental continuity between the systematic articulation of liberal ideology as in 'high culture' and the common-place symbolism to be found in popular culture and the world of everyday life. This continuity is reproduced through myths which dehistoricize the commonplace and empty it of all political significance. Instead of a counter-hegemonic symbolism, which is always a possibility given the social organization of everyday life round the social relations of production, through a texture of myths and other signs, common sense experience is pervaded with a sense of timelessness and innocuousness which serves to reinforce the prevailing order and the hegemony of the bourgeois class.

Barthes lays special emphasis on the role of the petit bourgeoisie in the reproduction of this ideological matrix. Whilst all classes in bourgeois society are to a greater or less extent hegemonized (see, for example, the influence of social reformism in the ideology of the working class) the strongest support from any other class for the bourgeoisie emanates from the petit bourgeoisie. Whilst they have none of the objective economic security of the bourgeois class, given their non-ownership of the means of production, they cannot claim any direct common interests with the working class either, given their non-involvement in productive labour. They therefore have an ambivalent class position which tends to lead to what might be termed an overcompensation within the sphere of ideology. As Barthes says:

> The bourgeoisie ceaselessly absorbs into its ideology a whole
> humanity which has none of its fundamental status, and can only
> live in it in their imagination, that is, through a fixation and
> impoverishment of consciousness. By spreading its representations
> across the whole catalogue of petit bourgeois images, the middle
> class sanctions the illusory lack of differentiation between social
> classes. (1972, p. 140)

But this is not a process which leaves bourgeois culture intact. On the

111

contrary, as Coward and Ellis argue in their discussion of Barthes:

High culture is extended and vulgarized into a kind of public philosophy. The innovatory and exploratory aspects in bourgeois thought are eliminated: the petit bourgeoisie cannot comprehend the other, that which exists outside its realm and defines the limits of that realm. The petit bourgeois world is the world of sameness, of endless repetition of identical forms, the world of so-called mass culture.

This alleged vulgarization or bastardization of bourgeois high culture forms a central theme in many of the contemporary controversies in education. The lament for the decline of the liberal university in the face of a growing pragmatism and utilitarianism reflects in great part the changed social role of the university from a status differentiating institution for the aristocracy and the old professions to a training locale for the masses of specialized functionaries required by more complex and differentiated capitalist productive systems. This trend has had important significance for the petit bourgeoisie who rely on their education to preserve their distinctiveness *vis à vis* the working class and on their 'knowledge' for their labour power, but it has had the consequence of diluting the social cachet which used to follow from an initiation into an esoteric high culture. Similarly, the concern over standards in the primary and secondary schools reflects in some way a bourgeois class on the defensive against the apparent erosion of its culturally hegemonic position in the realm of ideas but also concerned about the assault on traditional social relations in education which is thought in some way to be contributory to these 'declines' in some social formations, educators have articulated significant anti-both these areas for undermining traditional bourgeois culture.

An analysis of the class position of the petit bourgeoisie is important for anyone interested in education as an ideological apparatus (Ahier, 1977). Teachers are usually salaried employees of the state which defines them as petit bourgeois in class location. Their intermediate position in the social relations of production explains how, in some social formation, educators have articulated significant anti-capitalist ideologies (in contemporary France and Italy, for example, or in parts of Latin America), whilst at other conjunctures many have provided strong social support for reactionary political positions – in fascist Japan and Nazi Germany.

Petit bourgeois ideology, with its accompanying themes of ontological anxiety, exaggerated commitment to individualistic competitiveness, and its conceptualization of social hierarchies as open, natural and just, is significant for comprehending the class perspective of many educators. But it is not an ideology which instills self-confidence. Petit bourgeois educators have been unable to develop an autonomous educational ideology reflecting a separate identity and independent class interests. With the development of mass education the petit bourgeoisie lies increasingly unhappily between the bourgeois class who are its masters and other subordinate classes who (arguably) mistakenly look to education as the key to their social improvement.

An escape from ideology?

These developments in the Marxist theory of ideology have demonstrated that the individual subject is not the sole source or even the most important source of his own thoughts. Thoughts are mediated through language and ideology: 'Any cognitive thought whatever, even one in my consciousness, in my psyche, comes into existence as we have said, within an ideological system of knowledge where that thought will find its place' (Volosinov, 1973, p. 35). Ideas are thus embedded in and interpreted through ideology. Moreover, since ideology is enclosed within a system of material practices and routines and does not just consist of thoughts, concepts and theories, the political and educational problem of the conditions under which people could become self-consciously aware of the nature of their ideologies, their social genesis and function, is of crucial importance. It is clear that a model which explains changes of consciousness in terms of mere reason, argument and logical discourse is quite inadequate. There is a reciprocal interaction going on all the time between ideas and the practices and rituals which support and help to reproduce them such that, to expect someone to change his way of thinking when his whole 'experience' contradicts it, is overtly optimistic.

Marx was a product of the European rationalist tradition in which reason was seen as the sole basis for thought, and which ignored the extent to which much of our ideological practice is itself unconscious. Our thought involves thinking *within* our assumptions rather than thinking *about* them. How can we intellectually change our ideas when we have not even begun to think self-consciously about our practice in the world and its taken-for-granted assumptions? We may 'hear' new thoughts, but, indeed, our interpretation of them will

113

depend upon where we are located ideologically at the time. Those new ideas will not necessarily mean to us what the speaker intended them to mean. Meaning is always built up in a context containing other signs, and in a non-verbal situation which is itself infused with meaning. What in any case does it mean to think? It may be that our defining criterion of what it means to think is itself very historically specific and refers to a very narrow type of thought and thinking, itself a product of a class society where there is a division between mental and manual labour, and where some live for and from the pursuit of ideas. Such people will have been socialized to examine systematic bodies of thought for their internal consistency, logical coherence and so on. It is their type of thinking that provides the model for thinking 'in general'. However, it is well known that even mental labourers, when thinking about issues which are not normally the subject of academic theorizing – how to organize the division of labour within the family, how and whether to discipline their children – often seem to exist conceptually within all sorts of apparent contradictions that are both tolerated and indeed probably functionally necessary, given the conflicting nature of what is expected of them. We suggest here that the thinking characteristic of living in the world of 'everyday life' may be characteristic of most people's thinking, even of those who specialize in it. It would certainly not satisfy any rigorous criteria of rationality.

Furthermore, the range within which individuals think spontaneously and produce genuinely new thoughts may be very narrow. Letters in popular newspapers, for example, radio talk-back programs, or middle-class dinner parties often give evidence of people apparently communicating to each other, but saying nothing new. Their communication consists of elaborate, stereotypical, routinized utterances where the content is highly predictable, indeed, known in advance – a complex self-sustaining repertoire of conceptual formulations which provide little intellectual space for genuine thought. Our ideas are already pre-packed for us by our language and stereotypes built into the language in such a way that the possibility of thinking outside these very narrow limits is remote or haphazard.

If the aim is to encourage people to be self-conscious about their assumptions, to critically compare the contents of their thoughts and to rationally contrast and appraise alternative models of how social reality is constituted, then, clearly, the Marxist theory of ideology will have certain policy implications. First, that changes in thoughts must simultaneously be accompanied by alterations of the practices and routines which help to sustain those outmoded thoughts; we cannot retain the material practices of another practical ideology with much hope of blending them with an alternative message. Second, it requires that we identify the potential fissures in people's practical ideologies, the points at which the inner contradictions in these formulations can be most easily brought to consciousness. Third, it necessitates an attempt to build alternative organizational forms through which a counter-hegemonic consciousness can be produced: simply to rely on existing institutions may accentuate the problems, given the extent to which these forms will already have been infused with bourgeois hegemonic meanings. Fourth, given the unconscious nature of much ideology, it might be appropriate to take a few lessons from the psychoanalytic practice of therapy aimed at assisting people to come to terms with and recognize the contents of the unconscious. One obviously cannot ignore the mechanisms for the defence of the psyche and just announce an alternative authoritative message. It has to be recognized that people are already ideologized and cannot just be taught how inadequate their ideologies are, given that their ideologies are *their lives*, and to an important extent *themselves*. Finally, given the major contradiction between the private appropriation of capital and the collective nature of work, the more people's collective experience of living and working jointly with others is utilized, the easier it will be to penetrate the fetishized forms of bourgeois individualism, the basis for the dominant ideology. All these issues will be taken up more explicitly in relation to education in the final chapter.

115

5 Ideology and schooling

In the previous chapter the elements of Marx's theory of ideology and some of the more recent developments in the Marxist tradition were outlined. It is now possible to show how concepts emanating from that discussion can be applied fruitfully to the analysis of schooling and the 'knowledge' which educational institutions transmit. The concept of ideology will play a crucial role in clarifying the way in which schooling functions to reproduce the social relations of production, or the class relations within society, as well as generating some of the tensions and contradictions which are a necessary consequence of the logic of capitalist development. Nevertheless a major qualification is necessary. However important the role of schooling, other institutions or apparatuses as well are involved in these processes. Any systematic account of the ideological function of education has to locate education within a more comprehensive theoretical framework which takes cognizance of the complex ideological mediation occurring within such institutions as the family, the media, the churches, and trade unions, as well as within the day-to-day routines of capitalist work processes and within the forms and practices of the capitalist state. A whole network of institutions and practices articulate with those which characterize what is normally understood as schooling.

The contemporary form of schooling in capitalist societies is the result of historical processes and struggles. The accumulation process in any social formation structured by the capitalist mode of production is characterized by certain phenomena which occur generally. These combine with more idiosyncratic features of its development and the class struggle in particular socio-historical conjunctures to produce the specific characteristics of each national educational system. However, whilst schooling in general tends to reproduce capitalist social relations, it does not follow that it can do no other, that the mechanisms and ideological forms through which this end is achieved are invariant, or that the process of ideological reproduction occurs without simultaneously reproducing or reflecting the contradictions which latently are inherent in any capitalist society. This contradiction is related to the tension between the private appropriation of capital and the increasing socialization of production. It is important to avoid a timeless functionalism and an invariant teleology, for reasons which will be elaborated briefly in the next chapter in the context of a brief discussion of the inadequacies of Althusser's analysis of the ideological role of schooling.

In the previous chapter, it was suggested that the reproduction of capitalist production relations necessarily entails a process of maintaining hegemony. We have seen how hegemony can never be presumed in the context of class struggle but has to be fought for. This is so even where, on the surface of its operations, capitalist society seems to be functioning in a stable, ongoing, tension-free manner. The analysis will begin by a discussion of the history of British education in the last 200 years which provides an illustration of the changing forms and content through which hegemony has been achieved as well as illustrating many of the concepts concerning the relationship between schooling and ideology.

The three crucial issues concerning education from both a political and a theoretical perspective are those of content, control, and access. The question of access will only be examined here in terms of the ideological consequence of differential access to formal schooling and the shifts in the ideological plane which have led historically to a preoccupation with access issues. More interesting are the connected issues of content and of where control over schools resides, both of which influence and to some extent structure the form of class and other struggles over schooling.

Class struggles for hegemony. Who controls the schools?

The provision of universal state education reflects a resolution of the question of control over the schools in favour of the dominant classes whose interests are articulated in the apparatuses of the state and in their functioning. That control is now exercised through a variety of means: by the financial provisions of the state educational system through central or local taxation, by the legal requirement for parents to ensure that their children attend school, and by the state either directly or indirectly, being the main employer of teaching personnel, and by controlling the forms and content of professional training which determine the criteria of qualified teacher status. Moreover, control is further facilitated by the fact that mass schooling has everywhere taken the form of education in specialized institutions for children, separated from the world of work and from other adults, many of whom are thought to be incapable of exercising an appropriate educative influence on the young. As a result, there is an inbuilt bias in the ideological content of education towards the reproduction of hegemonic meanings and practices. This situation was not brought about, however, by a smooth struggle-free process. Nor has the class accommodation achieved by universal mass state education prevented any further resurgence of struggles over content and control in later periods although it may have affected their manifestations. This illustrates the point made in Chapter 4 concerning the delicate status of hegemony and the continuing need, on the part of the dominant classes, to struggle to maintain it.

A fascinating illustration of this process can be found in England in the period from 1789 to the early 1840s, as recent historical work on education has shown (Johnson, 1976; Silver, 1965; Simon, 1960; Harrison, 1961, 1968; Thompson, 1965, among others). Other significant periods of educational controversy over similar issues occurred at the end of the nineteenth century, in the 1920s and 1930s, and at the end of the long boom in the post Second World War period. Such struggles seem to have coincided with periods of downturn in the capital accumulation process when the ongoing threat to hegemony is likely to be more overt. The earlier period, for example, was an era which was dominated by the aftermath of the French Revolution, its attendant political and economic problems and the crisis of hegemony which these conditions engendered. It was also characterized by the rapid transition from machine industry to factory based production, the implications of which will be elaborated upon later. At the political level there was a heightened manifestation of class consciousness, political activity and organization, reflected in Owenism and the Chartist movement on the one hand, and in the changing alliances between landed and industrial capital, with respect to the Corn Laws and the Factory Acts, on the other. A counter-revolutionary reaction was the main feature of political events during these decades and provides the essential background against which to understand the struggles over education. It was during this period that the main features in the pattern of public educational provision, including the trend towards the increasing predominance of the state, were laid down, which set the parameters within which subsequent debate over the form and pattern of education would be conducted (Johnson, 1976).

The 1830s was the crucial decade. When it began, there was essentially what amounted to a dual system of education competing for the allegiance of the working class. On the one hand, there existed a whole network of strongly based, self-consciously working-class institutions with their own autonomously developed traditions of self-education independent of middle-class control, a network which had already produced a stratum of what Gramsci called 'organic intellectuals' (Gramsci, 1971) who were articulating the demands of the working class and influential in developing its various political strategies. Many examples of these institutions are discussed in E.P. Thompson's seminal study *The Making of the English Working Class* (1965). They include the radical press, corresponding societies, trade unions, radical sunday schools, Chartist and Owenite schools and halls, as well as numerous spontaneously generated reading and discussion groups unattached to any specific organization. Functioning parallel with these specifically working-class organizations, on the other hand, were the more conservative sunday schools, factory schools, and monitorial schools, essentially provided by sections of the middle class *for* the working class, together with some institutions specifically for adults such as the mechanics institutes, and others pioneered by such organizations as the Society for the Diffusion of Useful Knowledge (Shapin and Barnes, 1977).

Naturally, the rhetoric and intentions of the two systems differed. In both, however, the political and ideological functions were recognized as paramount and their class role as relatively unambiguous.

Simon has outlined the main themes of the former tradition which combined a critique of existing educational provision with a radical political and socio-economic perspective (Simon, 1972). Arising out of the European rationalist movement of the eighteenth century, articulated by such writers as Tom Paine and William Goodwin, they were based upon a belief in the formative power of education and the liberating potential of science and reason. Knowledge would dissolve the ideological mythologies of the past, such as religion, and, more significantly, serve as an instrument for achieving social, political and economic justice. Johnson (1976-7) has described how these themes developed into quite a sophisticated social science of ideology and the class role of the state in safeguarding the institutions of private property. Within Owenism, for example, education was seen as strategic class instrument in the struggle to achieve emancipation from oppression and the transformation of society into a more humane and educative environment (Harrison, 1968). In no sense was education regarded as a thing. Rather, it was thought of as a process for and on behalf of the class which should be combined with a progressive pedagogy emphasizing collective rather than competitive individual effort, and common rather than private goals. Although the details of this radical tradition and its incorporation in specific institutional forms have still to be elaborated, sufficient is known already to establish it as beginning to achieve a sense of class consciousness and a working-class counter-hegemony that posed a threat to public order and the operation of a free market economy. Of course, the extent of this counter-hegemony should not be exaggerated. For many, sheer economic necessity to work for long hours on low rates of pay left little time to devote to reading and self-education. Moreover, given its location within the working class, there was a lack of finance and other resources for buildings, books and other necessities. However, it seems reasonable to suppose that if it had not existed, the timing and the form of state involvement in education might have been rather different from that which transpired. Given its obvious power, there was a clear and un-ambiguous need to re-establish a reconstituted hegemony, to bring about a radical re-alignment of class forces to incorporate more effec-tively an urban mass seen as getting out of hand.

As might be expected, the concerns of those educational institutions firmly under middle-class control were the direct political counterpart of those of the working class. The essential requirement was to restrain the working classes and train them in the habits of good order, respect for property and authority. In much of the middle-class rhetoric of the time, as employed by Kay-Shuttleworth, for example (Johnson, 1970), we find an indictment of patterns of working-class life, a sus-picion of working-class parents as adults who will almost certainly lead the young astray, politically and ideologically, and a preoccu-pation with establishing an appropriate organizational form which could provide an adequate substitute for working-class parents to effect an education (or rather, schooling) firmly under middle-class direction. The above themes are by no means specific to this period but have continued to dominate educational debates to this day. We can see this clearly in contemporary discussions of the education for the culturally deprived, or the socially disadvantaged, and in debates concerning the aetiology of violence in inner-city schools. The main aim was unequivocally social control, however it was disguised ideologically. It is not necessary to invoke a conspiracy theory to understand the pattern of events. From the developing bourgeois perspective, of course, the urban masses becoming self-consciously politicized were a very genuine threat to a social organization based on private ownership of production which promised freedom, self-development and increasing well-being, but failed to provide the conditions for their achievement. If the battle was already lost with adults who were regarded as quite beyond the pale, then it had to be fought with even more vigour over the children concerning whom some hope remained of salvation from such dangerous influences (Johnson, 1976).

Throughout this period, then, there was a contending battle between different class forces for control over the 'hearts and minds' of the people – a battle for hegemony. The key issues were those of control and content, the key consequence the stability, or otherwise, of the basis of social order, the institution of property and the private accumulation of capital.

Eventually the working class lost out. Many of its educational initiatives disintegrated in the face of a prolonged assault by the state in the 1830s and early 1840s, in many cases through overt coercion, given that the basis for a reorganized and reconstituted hegemony had not yet been firmly established. By the end of the period, with the defeat of Chartism, it had suffered a major setback of great significance for the trajectory of future class struggles in and over education. An entirely different context had been created, in which the fundamental fight for control would henceforth be much more difficult to sustain, and consequently, the potential for ideological incorporation of counter-hegemonic tendencies be that much greater.

By the end of the century the effects of the way the class struggle had been resolved in this period had fundamentally altered the terms in which debates concerning education were articulated. The overriding question was now not control, or content, but the widening of access to the state educational system for larger sections of the working class. Whereas in the earlier period education had been seen to be of crucial significance for the *collective* interests of the class, indissolubly bound to political ends, now there would be a more individualistic orientation. The debate had become depoliticized. Educational expansion was now supported for individual mobility. Equality of opportunity, not equality of outcomes became the slogan. Increasingly the educational system

121

became defined as a neutral instrument, to be open to working-class individuals of talent and motivation to give them the same range of careers as their bourgeois and petit bourgeois counterparts. Such is the effect of hegemony (Johnson, 1976).

The weakness of these new studies in educational historiography is the lack of analysis in terms of the political economy of the developing capitalist mode of production. To focus on the class struggles of the period and the changing patterns of class alliances is important but what educational history requires is a more self-conscious effort to relate these processes to the problem of the articulation of modes of production in conditions where the capitalist mode of production was becoming dominant. The struggles in England after the French revolution need to be explained in the context of the specific problems of capital accumulation in the 1820s and 1830s, and the more favourable objective conditions for their temporary resolution in the 1840s, 1850s and 1860s. An understanding of the operation of the law of value which produces the tendency for the rate of profit to fall, and the mobilization of counter-tendencies on behalf of the capital relation is a necessary framework within which to situate the analysis of education in the context of capitalist production. As was argued above, an intensification of class struggles within and about education seems to occur in the periodic restructuring crises which necessarily flow from the inner dynamic of capitalist development.

The role of the state is central in these restructuring crises which also tend to affect the delicate balance of hegemony. The above discussion illustrates well the importance of the state in establishing hegemony. This does not mean that all capitalists were happy with what transpired. Not all fractions of the capitalist class supported the increasing educational involvement of the state. The desire to school the working class conflicted in many cases with the demand for cheap labour supplies but the compromise in the Factory Schools system, set up to resolve these difficulties, was hardly successful. These divisions within the capitalist class were paralleled by similar conflicts of interests over the Factory and Mines Acts, concerning the question of female and child labour, as Marx so brilliantly discussed in *Capital*, volume 1. But the long-term interests of the capitalist class in general necessitated state intervention whatever the opposition of individual capitalists. These may sometimes dictate political and economic concessions which fly in the face of the immediate economic interests of small-scale capitalists.

The discussion also illustrates the interrelationship between consent and coercion in guaranteeing the conditions for continued capital accumulation. The day-to-day operation of ideological agencies like schools occur in a context of constraint and coercion which in 'normal' times, where hegemony is unthreatened, rarely needs to be exposed. However, the inseparability of these two elements of class dominance is revealed in the ongoing process of accommodation and incorporation which the maintenance of hegemony entails. So is the changing 'accenting', to use Volosinov's terms, of concepts like education which accompanies this dynamism. It was precisely because the working class put such faith in education, albeit under their own control, that they did not resist the expansion of state education. In so doing, however, the apparent separation of educational goals from politics was institutionalized, a function of bourgeois control over the forms and content of state educational provision bringing about a reconstitution of the ideological and hence political role of schooling. Education became now, for many fractions of the working class something foreign, a thing 'experienced as an alien form'. But the very universality of state educational provision also ironically reconstitutes the forms and processes of working-class resistance. Mass literacy is always a potentially radical influence. The attempt by the state to break down local working-class initiatives necessarily entails an initiation of the young into other more general forms of consciousness which transcend local, community-based class horizons. Gramsci's thought and life testifies to this. Whatever the ideological content of these different forms of social consciousness, some exposure to different value systems, some cognition that there are alternative ways of seeing the world, some experience of marginality and alien forms of social practice might be a necessary precondition, if not sufficient for escaping from ideology and penetrating the level of appearances, however powerful the structural supports for the world of appearances may be.

Practical ideology and contemporary schooling

In the previous chapter an argument was offered for the explanatory priority of the concept of practical ideology. Although the role of schooling in articulating and propagating theoretical ideologies will be discussed later, it should be emphasized here that it is largely through practical ideology that the school manages to secure the conditions for continued capital accumulation and the reproduction of capitalist class relations. The manner in which schools, classrooms and knowledge are socially organized, the material practices and routines through which learning and teaching takes place provide the socially significant context which mediates any explicit transmission of formal knowledge, concepts and theories. Practical ideology is thus analytically and historically prior. Before any teaching takes place at all we are taught what to be taught entails. Whilst teaching and learning can occur under a great variety of conditions as comparative anthropological evidence illustrates, there are certain historically specific elements of practical ideology in schools in capitalist societies which bear close examination. Through its workings a social imagery and a series of conscious and unconscious messages are transmitted which prepare students for the material practices and routines necessary for capitalist work processes in their various manifestations and in the habits and rituals of 'decent law-abiding citizens'. The social relations of schooling in a class-stratified society are thus the more visible forms of what is fundamentally a class relationship, a class relationship which is not itself transcended by consciously exposing the ideological role of the practical ideologies within schools which mediate it. Nor is that class relationship simply destroyed through the generation of alternative practical ideologies, for example, through democratic and egalitarian rituals and practices within the classroom, the articulation of a 'progressive' pedagogical practice, although a movement towards the latter must necessarily be an important element in the development of any counter-hegemonic practice.

How does practical ideology produce its ideological effect? Within the classroom, pupils are engaged in processes which legitimate and in the last analysis reinforce the concept of the teacher as *the* pivotal authority, having the power to structure the pupil's day, define what is to count as knowledge, regulate the patterns of interaction through exercising control over classroom norms and regulations, as well as over the allocation of rewards and punishment through the grading and classification system. Within these overall constraints, however democratic or permissive the teacher, pupils carry on their educational 'work' individually rather than collectively and are encouraged for their diligence, social conformity and deference to the teacher's authority. These social practices are ideologically legitimated by a variety of educational theories whose political content remains hidden from their adherents (Stevens, 1978).

These social relations of the classroom are reproduced at a higher level in the social organization of the school. However democratic the form of decision-making, institutionalized in school councils or regular staff meetings, there is always some degree of centralization of control located firmly at the purse strings, and an institutionalization of hierarchy which, however weak the boundaries, tends to preserve a basic asymmetry of power between teaching personnel and pupils. Moreover, just as staff and pupils are differentiated, both horizontally and vertically, so the practical ideologies associated with the explicit transmission of knowledge tend to reinforce its arbitrary division into a number of discrete subject areas or 'disciplines', each with its own methodological presuppositions and principles of organization. In spite of the movement towards more 'integrated' studies, and the redefinition of traditional subject boundaries, school knowledge is still often characterized by dichotomies which parallel the hierarchical differentiations of pupils: pure/applied, abstract/concrete, specialized/general, academic/vocational, etc. Those pupils defined as bright or able are initiated into a pure, abstract, specialized academic curriculum whereas those designated less able are relegated to receive an applied, concrete, explicitly vocational education.

The political content of education is an absent presence. Politics, if studied formally at all, is reconstituted as segments of civics or social studies courses. Only some disciplines are seen as having any ostensible political content and that content is thought to lie in the subject matter under study rather than in the theories of methodologies which appropriate the content or through the value free solutions to the problems under examination.

In the material practices which structure the transmission of the curriculum, knowledge and life are arbitrarily separated. Knowledge is thought to have an ongoing objective facticity which can be brought to bear in an *ad hoc* way on the problem of life in the movement towards a more relevant curriculum. What is regarded as a problem in real life is not seen as something which has already been constituted ideologically. Where 'real life' processes enter the curriculum at all, it tends to be life apprehended through the phenomenal forms that were discussed in the previous chapter. The interconnections and real relations which lie behind these phenomenal forms are not themselves rendered problematic. This can be illustrated in the trend towards introducing school leavers to the world of work and other problems of living in an 'advanced industrial society'. Visits to local factories and offices, discussions of how trade unions work, how to fill in income tax returns, etc., rarely raise basic questions about the nature of capitalist production as a historically specific mode, not necessarily eternal, without any alternatives or impossible to transcend (White, 1977).

The consequence of the operation of practical ideology within the schools are far-reaching, its ideological significance profound. Through its working, the division between mental labour and manual labour, the fundamental attribute of a class society, is consolidated, reproducing the separation between thinking and doing, planning and execution, between those who produce, and those who organize and are sustained by the productive labour of others. Moreover, the key elements of liberal ideology, a belief in individualism and equality of opportunity, are reinforced. People involved on a day-to-day basis within the practical routines of the classroom acquire an attitude to the stratification system and of their own place within it through their ideological incorporation into the surface of its operations. They imbibe an explanation of social hierarchies as functional, necessary and inevitable, and of their own and other's location within it as being due to differential competencies, motivation and aptitudes upon which the school sets its seal of approval or disapproval. Thus the class reproducing aspects of schooling remain hidden, the class inequalities legitimated in this way continue unrecognized. Within the classroom, pupils seem to receive their just rewards for intelligence and effort, just as in the wage labour system for which most pupils are destined, labour reaps its due recompense in the value equation (Bohm-Bawerk, 1975).

Practical ideology and the hidden curriculum

The discussion so far bears some resemblance to what sociologists have referred to as the hidden curriculum. Jackson, in his work on classrooms (1968), wrote of it as something

> which each student (and teacher) must master if he is to make his way satisfactorily through the school. The demands created by these features of classroom life may be contrasted with the academic demands – the official curriculum, so to speak, to which educators have traditionally paid most attention. As might be expected the two curriculums are related to each other in several important ways. Indeed many of the rewards and punishments which sound as if they are being dispensed on the basis of academic success and failure are really more closely related to the mastery of the hidden curriculum.

Jackson regards the hidden curriculum as relatively benign as does Dreeben (1977). In their view it provides the necessary preconditions for effective learning in the classroom and is in no sense discontinuous with the norms and values of adult society on which social order ultimately depends. Neither of them discuss the hidden curriculum in terms of its ideological and political significance in sustaining a class society (Dale, 1977). Deschoolers like Illich, and Reimer, on the other hand, have a more critical attitude to it because of the way it produces habits of passivity and social conformity, an unthinking consumerism and a stifling of man's essential individuality and humanity. However, although the deschoolers recognize the political consequences of its functioning, they have no concept of man's nature being constituted within an 'ensemble of social relations' (Marx). They are trapped in their idealist categories and lack any adequate political economy of education which would explain why the content of the hidden curriculum is a necessary aspect of capitalist social relations which cannot merely be wished away by a utopian commitment to deschooling (Gintis, 1972). Sharp and Green (1975) offer a more penetrating analysis of aspects of the hidden curriculum which takes account of the material conditions in which teachers work both within and outside the classroom, but their analysis is also deficient because of their failure to produce an adequate materialist account of ideology. Their use of the term is shifting and is largely synonymous with 'perspective' or world view. They have no account of ideology as itself having a material reality embedded in practices and routines, neither do they situate the growth of a progressive, child-centred pedagogy in the context of the changing dynamics of capitalist production.

Education and the labour process

The attempt so far has been to demonstrate a relationship between practical ideology in schooling and the reproduction of capitalist social relations, the creation of a compliant labour force and a law-abiding citizenry. It is not the case, however, that the social relations within schools directly mirror those in the factory or the work place. The emphasis on practical ideology was to throw doubt on the liberal notion that what schooling provides for the economic structure is a highly-skilled and educated labour force, schooling being the agency whereby the masses are trained in the advanced instrumental skills and knowledge necessitated by a technologically based society. That schooling *is* involved in the production of skilled technologists and science-based expertise is undeniable, but the vast majority of the labour force are not engaged in occupations where high level skill and scientific knowledge is called for. This is, arguably, true even for the most successful products of schooling, those who go on to some form of higher education, many of whom study courses whose direct relevance for their subsequent occupations is often minimal. Moreover, the relationship between educational qualifications and the occupational structure is more complex than has hitherto been thought (Hussein, 1976). Whilst schooling, through the distribution of educational qualifications differentiates and divides pupils and formally establishes or legitimates their competencies for jobs (and their incompetence for other jobs) it is not the educational system *per se* that channels people into jobs. The specific range of occupations, their differentiations and hierarchies are determined outside the educational system in the organization of the production process itself. Poulantzas, in this context, has made an important distinction between two aspects of the process of social reproduction: on the one hand, the reproduction of the agents or production – their moulding into different kinds of subjects – such as clerks, managers, productive labourers or capitalists, and on the other, the reproduction of places within the productive process (Poulantzas, 1975a). Practical ideology within schooling is centrally concerned with the former and only with the latter in so far as transformations of the labour process create new places which require agents to be reconstituted as new kinds of subjects to fill them. However, an understanding of the latter is a necessary prerequisite for comprehending the changing ideological form of schooling given that capitalist social formations necessarily embody an inbuilt dynamism which alters the nature of the labour market.

Some insights into this essential dynamism can be gained by Marx's analysis in volume 1 of *Capital* concerning changes in the labour process (Marx, 1974a). The essential precondition, historically, for capitalism was the separation of the labourer from the means of production. This occurred in England through the enclosure movement and the destruction of artisan production as the factory system developed. Marx analysed the various stages of this transition from simple co-operation, to machine industry based upon domestic subcontracting and the putting out system, through to the modern machine-based factory in which all sequences of the production process are concentrated. In so doing, he shows how gradually over time the merely formal ownership of the means of production by the capitalist becomes translated into a real subordination of the labourer in the labour process which is now objectively subordinated to capitalist control. Whilst technological advance is a necessary feature of capitalist production it is clear that the specific mode of organization of the modern office or factory is not dictated by technological prerequisites *per se*, but by the requirement for an organizational form that facilitated capitalist control over the labour force. Meanwhile the development of the factory system and the consequent destruction of the domestic and local economy was accompanied simultaneously by the phenomenon of large-scale urbanization which undermined the old mechanisms of social control based on the network of institutional ties characteristic of the pre-industrial economy. The concentration of the work force in factory-based production and the growth of new urban communities established meanwhile a material base for the development of a counter-hegemony among factory workers and their families. The earlier discussion on the genesis of state intervention in education has isolated this feature – the threat to social and public order wrought by the process of factory production and urbanization coupled with the crisis in hegemony which followed the aftermath of the French Revolution, as the key variable in the rise of state involvement in education. It has less to do with the demand for new skills and expertise as liberal theorists often emphasize, and far more to do with the ongoing crisis in public order. Education was important for involving the masses into a new and transformed hegemony creating in them a consciousness which left the capital relation untrammelled.

Braverman, in his discussion of changes in the labour process during the twentieth century, has developed the argument much further (Braverman, 1974). The key question from the point of view of capitalist profit is: who is to control the work force in the day-to-day operations at the work place? Education may be important in producing a potential labour force with the appropriate attitudes and familiarity with capitalist work routines but without effective control over the organization of work itself, the process of surplus value generation would be impeded. In a seminal discussion of the growth of scientific management, he shows how the development of hierarchies, divisions and fragmentations within the work force has been the result of a deliberate strategy to separate the activities of planning and execution such that the day-to-day functioning at the work place is subjected to managerial control, the labourer becoming in a very real sense the appendage to

129

the machine which Marx described so vividly in *Capital*. This is not the place to discuss the obvious cognitive impairment which accompanies such a process. Nevertheless, the internal divisions within the class of wage labourers which follow from such changes in the labour process are important and do have vital ideological significance. The material separation of the activities of the productive labourers from those of foremen, supervisors, technicians and white collar work of various kinds (wage labourers who take over the managerial function from the direct control of the capitalist) is increasingly legitimated by educational qualifications, an ironic consequence of the tendency towards deskilling necessarily entailed by the fragmentation of tasks which results from the subordination of work processes to capitalist control.

These changes in the material practices in the labour process, not due, it should be stressed, to any technological imperative *per se*, have important ideological consequences. Despite the importance of education as an ideological agency, the routines and rituals of the world at work where most are constrained through economic necessity to engage in wage labour for the greater part of their adult lives are analytically prior. The labour process itself should be seen as the dominant ideological locale and site of reproduction of the social relations of production.

What implication does this have for education? It is possible, of course, to draw parallels between differentiation in the work force, the horizontal and vertical divisions which characterize the places in the occupational structure and the process of differentiation within schooling, producing distinctions between pupils on the grounds of such criteria as 'ability', sex, or race, and a fragmentation and com-modification of knowledge, but to formulate a simple one to one correspondence would be overly crude (Hextall and Sarup, 1977). The generation of new economic places does not automatically call forth from the educational system the supply of appropriately trained subjects or agents to fill them. Nor in the ongoing dynamic of capitalist development is the smooth transition between schooling and work guaranteed. Capitalist production necessitates a continuing process of transformation of the productive base and a tendency to substitute capital for labour. This can be aptly illustrated in the present stage of the international restructuring of capitalism which is characterized by the trend towards increasing centralization and concentration of capitalist production and the geographical relocation of production activities into low wages economies. High levels of unemployment, especially among school leavers, reveals the tensions and structural dislocations between the operation of the economy and the functioning of the educational system. Whilst the latter may be required by the state to participate in the process of reconstituting the labour force and develop transformed modes of social integration, the school's role in maintaining hegemony is, by no means, without contradictory elements. Its operations reveal the complexity of the ideological domain. In the state apparatuses the imperatives of legitimating and guaranteeing the conditions for continued capital accumulation may conflict. In recent years these contradictions have been reproduced within the educational apparatus itself, reflected in the heated debates which have centred on it in the public arena. Nevertheless the school's role in reproducing the division between mental and manual labour is, so far, unimpaired. The development of capitalist forms of work organization necessitate the emergence of a legitimated differentiation between those who have the monopoly over the knowledge which is ostensibly required to 'think', plan, and innovate, and those who have been cast in the role of subjects who will simply execute decisions made elsewhere. As Poulantzas (1975a, 251–70) has pointed out, the real significance of education is the way it excludes the working class from mental labour, and distributes agents among the enormous variety of petit bourgeois occupations which the transformations in the labour process have generated. The special relationship of the petit bourgeoisie to knowledge, culture and the educational apparatus referred to in the previous chapter is inextricably bound to the changes in the organization of work which Braverman's discussion illuminates. The same processes throw light on why the educational system becomes a focus of public controversy when educational qualifications no longer guarantee a safe access to the world of employment in times of economic crisis.

Culture clash in the school

A useful distinction can be made between, on the one hand, the institutional incorporation of the working class into the forms and processes of capitalist schooling, and on the other, its ideological incorporation. Whilst universal education provided by the state ensures that the children of the working class spend a high proportion of their early lives in schooling institutions not under their control – i.e. institutional incorporation, and whilst this may be an important precondition for ideological incorporation, the latter can never be complete. It would involve a complete disappearance of any spontaneous forms of working-class social consciousness and the generation of a new practical ideology which was thoroughly structured and framed within the boundaries defined by the dominant hegemonic system. However, working-class pupils are not simply exposed to schools, but are also constituted as thinking and acting subjects within the family, peer groups and local community, each of which may generate different practical ideologies which do not always mesh satisfactorily with those that pervade schooling.

In progressive liberal theory a cultural explanation for the failure of working-class pupils compared with their middle-class counterparts is often invoked. The school is seen to be the site of a cultural clash where the working-class pupil, who has previously been exposed to different cognitive assumptions, values, accents, or language, is subordinated to a middle-class culture via middle-class teachers imposing their own conception of the good and the true on their pupils who have been very differently socialized. Such a theory has, typically, given rise to one of two variants: either working-class culture has been seen as inferior, deficient in some crucial respects, necessitating early cultural intervention to provide for these pupils what the middle class 'naturally' acquire, or alternatively it is seen as equally valid, with its own inherent integrity. Those holding the latter view think it morally repugnant to repudiate the working-class child's own culture, the school should attempt to operate within it. In so doing the school can play its part in producing a genuinely pluralistic, multi-cultural society. They believe that teachers should be educated to be more sensitive to working-class culture, avoid its denigration and appreciate its educative potential and its own inner aesthetic. A great debate has taken place over the concept of cultural deprivation (Freedman, 1967; Keddie, 1973 and Flude and Ahier, 1974) and the underlying assumptions of the model have been fully exposed. However, regardless of the stance taken towards the issues of 'deprivation' or 'differences', most liberal theories of education ascribe the educational difficulties of the working-class pupil to differences in their culture and explain the class reproducing aspects of education as being in some way centrally concerned with cultural clashes.

The bourgeois notion of culture, however, differs quite significantly from the Marxian concept of ideology (Williams, 1977b). The former tends to lead to a sociology of meanings, norms, attitudes and values with little reference to any practical or material base. From within a Marxist perspective, such a concept has little explanatory power. Far from culture being the basic causal category, what needs to be explained is the content of that culture, its material embeddedness in concrete social practices, its socio-historic genesis and its causal efficacy (Clarke *et al.*, 1976). Moreover, a Marxist would be sceptical of the idea of a multicultural, pluralistic society in the absence of an appropriate material base, given that class societies are structured by different social relations of production and asymmetry in the distribution of economic and political power. It is true that the school is a site of differences in class cultures or ideologies but these class cultures or ideologies are not, analytically or concretely, separable from each other. Using the concept of hegemony, it is clear that it is not middle-class culture but the dominant hegemonic ideology which is being transmitted in schools. As a result of the process of incorporation discussed in the previous chapter, the hegemonic ideology contains elements not simply from the bourgeois class, but also from the landed aristocracy, and reconstituted and incorporated elements from the ideology of subordinate classes. Moreover, the supposedly spontaneous ideology of the working class is itself penetrated by notions, practices and routines emanating from the hegemonic system. This is precisely what hegemonic dominance means. Thus, it is through this class ideology that the working class lives its subordination in society and that process of subordination involves also a subordination at the level of ideas and practical ideologies. What happens in schools is not the imposition of a middle-class culture on other groups whose own culture is quite alien, but a process of further ideological incorporation of the subordinate classes. However, although working-class ideology is already articulated with and permeated by the meanings and practices of the hegemonic ideology it always embodies contradictory elements, given that there are aspects of working-class social relations which are still insulated from capitalist control. It may well be that the shifts in class relations which are occurring, due to the reshaping of the productive base which forms the material and social context of many working class communities, are bringing about a weakening of the traditional supports for working-class 'culture' and its potential for oppositional counter-hegemonic tendencies. Such a process has been accentuated by housing redevelopment which often alters the pattern of social life and renders more precarious the supportive bonds derived from the spatial coexistence of family, work and living community. The growth of the mass media and other electronic forms of communication has also had an influence, although the ideological content of the media is mediated by the varying forms of social consciousness of its audience and the structured material and social processes conditioning its reception (Williams, 1974). However, despite these disruptive trends, there is little reason to anticipate the total demise of what E.P. Thompson has called the 'warrening from within' the hegemonic ideology, even if the forms of warrening may differ, being more self-consciously apolitical, and privatized than before (Thompson, 1965).

School cultures and subcultures

A Marxist analysis of the ideological role of schooling does not therefore imply a model of the school pupil as an over-socialized, completely ideologized responder to forces beyond his control. Schools also, it needs to be emphasized, produce and reproduce distinctive patterns of opposition which mediate their ability ideologically to incorporate successfully all those who pass through them. Sociologists have often pointed to the effects of specific organizational processes, of patterns of grouping students, or organizing knowledge and pedagogy in generating subcultures within the school which distort or undermine its working (Hargreaves, 1967; Lacey, 1970). Members of the Birmingham Cultural Studies Centre have recently been developing the concept of youth subculture within a Marxist problematic and have offered a range of suggestive insights which could be applied creatively to the analysis of youth subcultures within schools (Hall and Jefferson, 1976). They define culture as an active process of producing meanings in determinate conditions of which those arising from the elementary division of labour at the level of production are regarded as primary. Different class cultures or subcultures thereof are related to different class positions and are seen as a material expression of class interests generated therefrom. However, the ideological manifestation of these common class interests may vary, partly because, although there may be a common class problematic which cannot easily be transcended, a similar range of objective conditions which structure the main parameters of social existence, these objective conditions do not always impinge at the same time, in the same way, through the same mechanisms or with the same force, upon all members of the class simultaneously. Using this framework they have attempted to study the various subcultural forms within young working-class peer groups which, in their terms, 'resolve ideologically, in an imaginary way, the real relations which cannot otherwise be transcended'. These ideological resolutions are articulated with the ideological content of the parent culture (that of the working class with respect to mods, rockers, and skinheads; that of the middle-class or the petit bourgeoisie with respect to the counter-culture). However they also provide some creative reconstitution of the parent culture. Berkoff's play, *East* provides a brilliant analysis and implicitly Marxist critique of traditional working-class life, showing its energetic wastefulness and the imaginary forms through which the problems of life are confronted and mediated in London's East End, depicting simultaneously the timeless preoccupations of the class as a whole and their variants among young people. A semiotic analysis of the style, the rituals, the language and gestures explore the important ways in which subcultural ideology produces its effects – but that it *has* an ideological effect is undeniable. Now schools help to create the conditions for the reproduction and accentuation of these ideological forms through their own ways of working. They gather together young people from largely similar backgrounds grouping them together in the same territorial surroundings. The material conditions for a creative subcultural response is there. The process of ideological incorporation, or lack of it, of the working class into schools cannot be understood via a psychologistic model focusing on the individual teacher and student alone. Many young working-class pupils in schools confront simultaneously both the denial of educational opportunity via the labelling process plus the prospect of alienating work situations or, increasingly frequently, no prospect of work at all. The geographical relocation of industrial production has added to the consequences of the long-term rise in the organic composition of capital leaving in its wake a likelihood of continued structural unemployment for many who have already been defined as failures in schools. Faced with these objective conditions it is hardly surprising that collective responses are generated, responses which are no more immune from the influence of hegemonic beliefs and practices as the content of the class culture of their parents. Now it is important to understand these ideological forms and the role they play in mediating directly the experience of schooling as well as articulating with the life lived outside it. Paul Willis has made some important starts to this analysis in *Learning to Labour* (1978). The importance of his work justifies more than the citation in this chapter.

It is without doubt the most significant contribution to the study of schooling which has been published for many years.[1] It illustrates the creativity of the collective work being carried out at the Birmingham Cultural Studies Centre where Willis is based and the absolute necessity of a well-developed theoretical perspective for any penetrating ethnography. Facts do not speak for themselves, they have to be theoretically defined and interpreted.

The phenomenon that Willis sets out to explain is why, in the context of a class society, some working-class pupils voluntarily choose to lock themselves into apparently personally unrewarding and low status manual labouring jobs, despite a schooling system which ostensibly provides some opportunities for social mobility and despite a genuine concern on the part of many of their teachers and youth employment officers to rescue them from that fate. In Marxist terms, the book is concerned to explore some aspects of the process of social and cultural reproduction.

Using an ethnographic case study of a group of working-class youths from an all-male comprehensive school in an English industrial conurbation, he raises vitally important questions about the way in which the themes within their subculture, a subculture which is continually being actively created and reconstituted with all its inner spontaneity, tensions and contradictions, decisively reflects and helps to reproduce the lived experience of these pupils both within and outside the school. In short, the 'lads' are anti-school. They reject the individualistic and competitive ethos which pervades capitalist education. They eschew intellectual work and resist the official rationales and justifications for the way things are. Instead they substitute their own meanings, rituals and pastimes which have little to do with what schooling has to offer. If he had stopped there, Willis would have provided few new insights, only additional, often juicy, evidence to support what every sensitive teacher has known since the onset of mass schooling: schools are arenas where a losing battle is being waged for the 'hearts and minds' of the working class. Teachers of the working class confront a class culture which is alien from and often antagonistic to everything

---

[1] It should be compared with Madan Sarup's *Marxism and Education* (Routledge, 1978) which is simplistic and, from many points of view, fundamentally misleading in that he relies heavily on Aviniri's and Ollman's interpretation of Marx. Sarup lacks, for example, a coherent theory of ideology and of the capitalist state and neglects many aspects of Marx's mature work, in particular the analysis of the capitalist reproduction process as set out in vols 1–3 of *Capital*.

the school tries to impart. It subverts their aims and undermines their good intentions.

The distinctiveness of Willis's work is that he provides an analysis of how these apparently oppositional and antagonistic attitudes towards schooling are vitally important components of the way in which the class structure is legitimated and sustained through time. The themes within the subculture, linked as they are with broader aspects of working-class experience outside the school, in reality work to sustain the existing patterns of domination and subordination within society and the framework of capitalist production. For example, he describes the 'lads' opposition to and contempt for the 'ear-oles', the conformist pupils who work hard and aspire for individual mobility, their upturning of the usual way of ranking mental and manual labour, through their celebration of masculinity and physical prowess, and shows how these serve precisely to perpetuate and reinforce that very distinction between mental and manual labour which is an important aspect of the legitimation of class inequality under capitalism. Similarly he reveals the way in which the sexist and racist themes within the anti-school subculture reflect and reproduce the divisions within the working class which Braverman's seminal work, discussed earlier, has demonstrated to be an essential aspect of capitalist control over the labour process and the work force. More importantly, he provides a way of theoretically linking these two insights through his observation that the 'lads' define mental labour, the destiny of most of the 'ear-oles', as essentially cissy, effeminate and inferior. He thus links patriarchy and capitalism in an original way. In brief the book is documenting the manner in which the very mode of the lads' resistance to the received wisdom of schooling precisely prepares them for their future insertion into the social and ideological practices of the shop floor, in fact, for an *acceptance* of manual labour in a social world which at least partially they have learned to reject. For example, they will have nothing to do with the middle-class notions of vocational choice propagated by the school which emphasize the need to match individual aptitudes and motivations against the variety of vocational satisfactions emanating from a horizontally and vertically differentiated job market. They perceive, quite rightly, that most jobs are routine, boring, oppressive and alienating, even those entailing mental labour. Nevertheless their subculture does not enable them to link this insight with the essential nature of capitalist production and the variety of mechanisms which help to maintain it. Instead it locks them into manual labour and the world of appearances in a manner which ideologically assists in its reproduction. Willis's study is deeply and pervasively informed by a theoretical analysis of the nature of capitalism as a system and a sophisticated theory of ideology which depends heavily on the work of Gramsci, in particular, the latter's discussion of the contradictory nature of commonsense. Although Willis does not avail himself of the concept of hegemony, the two crucial analytical concepts that he uses to interpret the structure of the lived experience of his subjects: penetrations and limitations, derive from a notion of hegemonized common sense. 'Penetrations' can be illustrated by the earlier discussion of the 'lads' attitude towards vocational choice. Willis is arguing that to some degree and in a partial way these lads see through the surface of bourgeois society, penetrate its observable manifestations and discern at least some aspects of the structure of inequality and demystify the institutions which help to reproduce it, like the school. However, these partial glimpses are foreclosed and foreshortened by 'limitations' which prevent them from discerning the whole nature of capitalism for what it is, a system of class domination based upon the appropriation of surplus value emanating from their own labour power. In other words, common sense, always a potentially radical force when things are not as they seem to be, is structured by and intersected with dominant or hegemonic meanings and practices which mask the real structure of class domination. He also provides a non-mechanistic view of how ideology works, by being actively constructed and reconstituted through the ongoing apparently oppositional lifestyles of youths such as the subjects of his study, resulting in a mode of existence in adult life which is precisely what capitalism requires.

I have summarized the book in some detail because, despite its importance, it is not easy to understand. Whilst written in a clear, concise and dense style, the language he uses is complex and often technical and he has paid insufficient attention to the problems of his audience. If this is a book which every radical teacher should read, is it written in a way that facilitates the grasping of the ideas? The answer, I am afraid, has to be no. Perhaps what is required is the establishment of *Learning to Labour* reading groups where the ideas could be discussed collectively and an effort made to work through the pedagogical implications.

Willis's study needs to be replicated elsewhere. All capitalist societies share some common features relating to the need to produce for profit and sustain a system of class domination. However, as we have suggested, the specific course of capitalist development and the trajectory of class struggles has varied historically over time in different national contexts. It may well be that there are specific features of capitalism within other societies and the manner of the ideological incorporation of the working class which would substantially modify Willis's analysis. To what extent, for example, has the heavy post-war reliance on migrant labour for manual work in countries like Australia and Sweden affected the way in which hegemony operates among the non-migrant working-class population? Willis's analysis also needs to be developed through additional studies of girls, of the 'ear-oles', and of schools experimenting with a radically different mode of pedagogy. One of the problems here is that educational research funding bodies have not shown themselves very willing to support either basic theoretical work or studies which reject a positivistic methodology in favour of more qualitative, ethnographic, hypothesis-generating approaches. *Learning to Labour* surely provides a paradigm example of why such research is worthwhile.

An additional point which needs to be stressed is that Willis's study was completed at a time when the phenomenon of widespread youth unemployment was not figuring prominently. In England now and elsewhere, the typical destiny for unqualified school leavers is not productive labour, but the prospect of long-term, structurally induced unemployment. What implications will this have for schools and the content of the anti-school subculture, especially given the increased emphasis being given to vocational guidance and work experience in schools in many western societies. What implications derive from bodies such as the Manpower Services Commission? More importantly, what attempts will be made by the bourgeois class and the bourgeois state to ideologically contain the working class and the young as the recession proceeds?

It would be unfair to expect one book to resolve all the significant issues. Nevertheless if there is one main weakness in Willis's book it is his neglect of the role of the state in managing the transition from school to work. As our analysis has suggested, there is a need for further exploration of the nature of the capitalist state which becomes especially salient in times of economic recession. The ideological constitution of the crisis by the state, its modes of intervention into schooling, are decisive objects of the theoretical analysis of education which Willis tends to underplay. This is especially critical since behind the state's ideological interventions is a coercive power, a coercive power which in many capitalist societies is increasingly being used

139

not simply against those who voluntarily submit to manual labour, like the lads in *Learning to Labour*, but also against those teachers who are committed in their educational and political practice to subvert the mystifications which pervade capitalist schooling and offer something of more lasting value to their pupils.

The book is simultaneously pessimistic and optimistic. It both identifies the nature of the obstacles which prevent a greater awareness of how society works, and how these are sustained in the lived experience of working-class life, but it also reveals that working-class subculture is not locally hegemonized, but comprises themes and contradictions which can theoretically be built upon by radical teachers. However, I do not think that the analysis has yet been done which can guide us very much in the practice of Marxist pedagogy. The goals are clear but radical teachers lack a theory of pedagogy and are forced to rely on little more than hunches or intuitions. As I shall argue, this is an urgent theoretical and political task for Marxists and for educators. It entails in particular a Marxist theory of language, since language is one of the significant vehicles through which ideological shifts can be brought about. Willis tells us a lot about what one is up against but does not resolve the problem of pedagogy.

The kind of research being developed at the Birmingham Cultural Studies Centre, of which Willis's has, however, given rise to vocal criticism, especially from Althusserians of various kinds (Sparks, 1977; Coward, 1977). Coward suggests that an essentially bourgeois notion of culture is being employed – which defines its components as basically the product of individual consciousnesses acting together and realizing meaning. From an Althusserian perspective, the work on cultural studies is seen to be premised within a framework of a subject/object problematic, and to be idealist rather than materialist in its underpinnings. Thus the real world exists out there and knowledge directly appropriates the real via the senses. The subject is seen to misrecognize or misappropriate the existential world thus retreating into ideology which is conceptualized as false consciousness. Coward believes that this framework exempts the individual from the processes of the structures; indeed, the individual is defined as the origin and source of them. The critics want to displace a notion of consciousness as primary. Instead they advocate the use of Lacan's idea of the topology of consciousness structured through language which they believe accounts better for the process by which the effect of consciousness is constituted. Whatever the merits of some of these arguments, what is really at issue seems to be the precise relationship of class to ideology. The Althusserians would carry more weight if they went beyond calling for the production of the appropriate concepts with which to do analysis and proceeded to offer instead an alternative interpretation of these phenomena. Unless a movement is made beyond polemics against humanist Marxists and formalistic assertions, toward the concrete analysis of determinate conjunctures, the significance of Althusserian critiques of cultural studies like Coward's remains hidden in its unnecessarily elitist and obscure formulations. It necessarily excludes from its inner sanctums all but those who can master the appropriate jargon or who think the effort of doing so worthwhile.

Language, ideology and education

'When I use a word,' Humpty Dumpty said, in a rather scornful tone, 'it means just what I choose it to mean – neither more nor less.'

'The question is,' said Alice, 'whether you *can* make words mean so many different things.'

'The question is,' said Humpty Dumpty, 'which is to be master – that's all.'

Lewis Carroll, *Through the Looking Glass*
(quoted in Postman and Weingartner, 1971)

It is unnecessary here to engage in a critical evaluation of the contribution of linguistics and sociolinguistics to the analysis of the cognitive and social implications of the language used in schools. Useful overviews of the relevant issues have been published elsewhere. It seems important however, to make an intervention concerning the question of language as an important aspect of ideology.

In one of the most useful reviews of the controversy surrounding Bernstein's theories, Stubbs (1976) adopts what seems to be the dominant position in contemporary linguistic theory regarding different languages, dialects, etc., namely a culturally relativist stance that languages cannot be judged hierarchically in terms of their ability to realize cognitions. From the generalization that between and within different speech communities there are different norms which define appropriate language use – styles, speech variants, dialects, etc., he rejects a simple explanation of educational disadvantage in terms of a

141

concept of linguistic deprivation, and instead focuses attention on teachers' attitudes towards linguistic differences as the main explanatory variable, thereby invoking some notion of the self-fulfilling prophecy.

Educational disadvantage may be the result of people's ignorance or intolerance of cultural and linguistic differences. But such a disadvantage is not a deficit. I would thus reject the oversimple and dangerous catch phrase 'educational failure is linguistic failure', and substitute for it the more guarded statement: 'Educational failure often results from sociolinguistic differences between schools and pupils'. My own view is therefore as follows. 1) Schools and classrooms depend on language, since education as we define it in our culture is inconceivable without the lecturing explaining reading, and writing which comprise it. So if a school defines a pupil as linguistically inadequate then he or she will almost certainly fail in the formal educational system. (Stubbs, 1976)

Stubbs, thus, diverts the debate away from an idea of linguistic deprivation as a specific aspect of cultural deprivation towards a model which locates the onus of blame (if this term is appropriate) on the teacher. He stresses the need to analyse language within the context of the classroom as a system of social relationships between speakers and hearers, where the cognitive and social aspects of learning are inseparable.

The stress on attitudes to language and the explanation of educational failure as being produced by teachers' attitudes is, from a Marxist perspective, inadequate. Sharp and Green have materially grounded the analysis of the self-fulfilling prophecy to demonstrate how prophecies are generated and fulfilled in material conditions which impose a structure of constraints on teachers' freedom of action. Whilst Stubbs insists that language has to be viewed in the context of a social relationship between speakers and hearers and whilst he makes frequent reference to the concept of class, his analysis falls short because of his failure to conceptualize class as a production relationship existing outside the school. It is not possible to bracket out the whole of the social formation beyond the school and think of the linguistic relationship between speakers and hearers – teachers and pupils as merely an interpersonal relationship between individually constituted subjects. The focus for a theory of language in schools must be on the functioning of schools within a system of class relationships which are founded in the social relationships of production outside the classroom.

A cultural relativistic approach to language tends to obscure the relationships between dominant and subordinate classes and the processes of hegemonic practice which is realized, at least partly, through language. In addition it lends support to a rather naive view of the means whereby a hierarchical stratification in society can be eradicated, or at least equality of opportunity realized for those who do not speak standard English; namely, teach teachers the theory of the fundamental equality of all human languages and the irrationality of discriminating between pupils on the grounds of linguistic or any other criteria which reflect mere class differences rather than deficiencies.

Stubbs, however, strongly argues for an approach to the study of language in schools which goes far beyond a mere descriptive concentration on relatively superficial aspects of its surface structure. Rather than analyse isolated speech utterances in experimental situations, he advocates studies of linguistic discourse – i.e. sequences of concrete speech which occur with a regular form of ongoing social relationships. This is in line with Volosinov's stress on the way in which actual language usage in specific social and historical situations both 'reflects and refracts' but also constitutes, a particular view of the world and the social relationships therein; such a discourse analysis would attempt to elucidate the rules which structure educational dialogue and isolate the specific features of language which communicate messages regarding how knowledge and information should be organized and conceptualized, how debates and disagreements should be resolved, whether through appeals to reason, authority, experience or to 'what everyone knows'. Drawing on the work of Bellack *et al.* (1966), Sinclair and Coulthard (1975) and others, he discusses the issue of different types of messages transmitted by the sequencing and structure of the discourse, what is not said but communicated through extralinguistic signs, through the patterns of the utterances themselves and through the ongoing metacommunication – i.e. speech about the speech itself which often characterizes classroom discourse. Such studies are important for elaborating the mechanisms where pupils are constituted as subjects of different kinds within an overall ideological practice. But from a Marxist perspective they should be conducted within a model which gives explanatory priority to the context of speech, showing how different types of educational context are articulated with other contexts outside the school in the framework of the social relations of production characterized by definite relations of domination and subordination.

Agreeing with Stubbs, it is clear that 'different types of talk can sustain very different types of social relationships, and concepts of social order'. It is not merely in the content of what is actually said, but in the forms and structures of speech utterances, as a system, that social meanings and value judgments are produced and reproduced and the world constituted as a meaningful one. What is unclear from Stubbs's discussion, however, is the extent to which this process can be adequately understood without a concept of hegemony. The asymmetry of power involved in classroom talk, where control over the rules which structure classroom discourse resides with the teacher, provides the preconditions for the intrusion of hegemonic ideology into the pupil's consciousness. It is not, of course, a sufficient condition that the pupils are already constituted subjects before they enter school. They have also been exposed to specific forms of language usage sometimes at variance with that used in the school, which have realized an ideological effect, albeit not one free from hegemonic influences.

The class reproductive aspects of language usage in schools have been stressed: the way it is tied in with the social relations of production outside schooling, albeit mediated through a range of possible linguistic practices within different educational situations. It is, however, necessary to reassert the concept of language as an activity. If this language only ever does, can and could reproduce existing class relationships and if the person is constituted as a subject partly through language, then Saussure's distinction between signs and signals is rendered inconsequential. Words are not mere reflections of things and processes in the world out there – but signs, which do not by themselves determine what is signified. Because the meaning of a sign is worked through in social relationships and not external to them, the creative flux of language and its meaning is ensured. In educational debates we could give many examples of the dialectical flow of changing meanings of specific items of language: the concepts of 'knowledge', 'community school', 'parent participation', 'educational equality' are all examples of words or signifiers where what is signified has been open historically to a variety of interpretations and where, through specific struggles, some obvious shifts in meaning have occurred. The meaning of the term 'education' itself has never been unaccented, whatever the basic importance of such a word in the ongoing struggle to maintain hegemony.

Finally, a comment should be made about the relationship between specific forms of language usage and their implications or relationship to thought processes. Stubbs's conclusion seems at one level reasonable:

Throughout we have seen the complexities of the relationship between language and the social contexts in which it is used, and we have therefore seen that any simple causal model purporting to relate superficial aspects of language directly to educational processes will be oversimple. Superficial aspects of language would include accent, grammatical differences between standard and non standard dialects, the proportion of grammatically complex sentences a speaker uses and so on. There is no evidence whatsoever that such features of language are related, for example, to thought processes. (1976)

However, if one thinks of language as having not merely observable surface features but a deeper unconscious form or structure, it seems plausible that the further analysis of discourse will demonstrate that different types of discourse do have different implications for thinking and genuine communication. Whilst many of the criticisms of Bernstein's work as suggested by such writers as Labov (1973), Rosen (1972), Jackson (1974), Coulthard (1969) are sound, in its early stages of formulation, Bernstein's work offered a series of insights concerning the implications of different forms of language usage for the impairment of cognitive faculties. Too preoccupied with defending himself against the charge that his theory entailed a notion of working-class linguistic deficit (which it certainly did in its early formulation), and lacking any adequate theory of ideology, Bernstein missed the opportunity to pursue further the question of the relationship between speech and thought except in terms of the implication of different linguistic codes for thinking about different things, rather than thinking more coherently, or less coherently about anything. It follows logically from a Marxist theory of language and of ideology that it is both possible and politically necessary to make judgments about the adequacy of one's thought, otherwise the grounds for Marxism itself and its epistemological validity disappear. If Bernstein had persisted in his earlier insights instead of merely responding to what was primarily an ideological rather than a scientific attack on his work he might have been closer to showing the role of forms of language usage in the production of what Habermas has called 'systematically distorted communication', a process which in bourgeois society must pervade most forms of communication, not just that of the working class. In an ideal form of speech communication, there is no closure on the dialogue due to power, time or access to information. All validity claims are open to examination and need to be accounted for. In such an ideal discourse, the accidental or systematic constraints on discussion are non existent and the assumption is that through the process of argumentation and rationality, agreement can be arrived at (Habermas, 1970).

Now it is obvious that in class societies such conditions do not obtain nor can they. An ideal discourse is premised upon a situation of justice and equality between speakers, whereas most politically significant communciation takes place in contexts where there is an asymmetry of power to control the content, direction and outcome of linguistic interchanges. The implication of this for *what* people think about and *how* they think is important. Moreover, the notion of communicative competence in an ideal situation does provide a standard by which to judge actual speech situations and their likely cognitive consequences. As Habermas argued,

> The ideal speech situation is neither an empirical phenomenon nor simply a construct but a reciprocal supposition unavoidable in discourse. This supposition can, but need not be counterfactual; but even when counterfactual it is a fiction that is operatively effective in communication. I would therefore prefer to speak of an anticipation of an ideal speech situation. . . . This anticipation alone is the warrant that permits us to join to an actually attained consensus the claim of a rational consensus. At the same time it is a critical standard against which every actually realized consensus can be called into question and tested. (quoted by T. McCarthy, Introduction to Habermas, 1975)

In the light of this it is obvious that the specific patterns of linguistic discourse occurring in a class society generally, and in the educational system specifically, must be productive of a form of cognitive impairment or incompetence which ideologically legitimates and sustains the very conditions which render genuine rational communication rare, if not impossible.

Theoretical ideology and the content of the curriculum

The insistence on the analytical priority of practical ideology is supported by the fact that there are no examples in history of completely new systems of thought which develop in isolation from some preexisting changes in social arrangements. Thus the final content of the curriculum should be studied in relation to the social conditions in which knowledge is produced and reproduced over time and to the practical ideologies which these conditions generate. In addition, it seems reasonable to suggest that most of the schooled population encounter the content of the curriculum in the context of the rituals and practices which structure its transmission and rarely become initiated into the higher levels of theoretical ideology as coherent systems of thought. School knowledge is experienced as reified, fragmented and disparate collections of unproblematic 'facts'. The grounds of such knowledge usually remain hidden, the procedures for arbitrating between different knowledge claims rarely being exposed to critical examination. This applies not simply to practical ideology, the language, rituals and activities of common sense, but also to the higher levels of theoretical ideology which inform the content of the curriculum. In addition, it is often not recognized that (borrowing Marx's phraseology) 'behind the backs' of knowledge producers and consumers, are sets of social relationships which the form and content of theoretical ideology rarely expose or call into question. Thus within a framework of fetishized socia relations knowledge appears as somehow detached from its social basis and independent of its social function (Hextall and Sarap, 1977).

Since the 1960s there has developed a growing body of literature examining the social, political and value assumptions built into the different subjects which constitute the curriculum and the definition of what counts as legitimate knowledge within them. In the earlier discussion of the new sociology of the curriculum, relations of power and questions of social interest were stressed as necessary elements of a Marxist analysis of the content of the formal curriculum. However, idealist critiques of the presuppositions of different bodies of thought or demonstrations of their class function do not go far enough. What is required is an examination of theoretical ideologies in the context of the capital accumulation process and the class struggle in different social formations, its trajectory in relationship to the specificities of the development of the capitalist mode of production, using a comparative and historical framework. The differences in the content of theoretical ideologies which influence the nature of educational knowledge, cannot be understood without realizing the very different genesis of capitalism in different national contexts, the changing class compromises and alliances which were characteristic of that process, and the variations in the pre-capitalist mode of production with which the developing capitalist mode was articulating. In Britain, for example, there never was a fully-fledged bourgeois revolution which annihilated the landed aristocracy leading to the generation of an unmitigating bourgeois hegemonic dominance. What transpired instead was a reconstituted alliance between fractions of the landed classes and fractions of the bourgeoisie (the financial fraction based on the City of London) which was reflected in the content of the hegemonic ideology: an uneasy fusion between elements of bourgeois ideology and the ideology of pre-capitalistic feudal classes. As Nairn has put it: 'The English class compromise . . . was . . . the containment of capitalism within a patrician hegemony, which never, either then or since, actively favoured the aggressive development of industrialism or the general conversion of society to the latter's values and interests' (Nairn, 1977).

A useful comparison can be made with the situation in France where although the bourgeoisie became economically dominant, after the French Revolution when the aristocracy was annihilated, it was continually forced politically into class alliances with the peasantry and the petit bourgeoisie in order to counter the threat to its hegemony by the urban masses, especially in 1848 and 1870 (Marx, 1973a, 1973b). In Germany, on the other hand, the bourgeois class achieved only a very weak hegemony. Capitalism was fostered by an alliance between the large landed elements of the Junker class and fractions of the industrial and financial bourgeoisie, the former for long 'holding decisive political sway within this alliance' (Poulantzas, 1974) and the state playing a relatively greater role than in Britain or, to a lesser extent, France. There, too, the counter-hegemonic threat emanating from the urban proletariat was considerably greater, especially in the early years of the Weimar Republic.

Given these different historical conditions it is hardly surprising that the content of the hegemonic ideology in each country reflected these variations. Whilst in all three, the capitalist mode of production has been unmistakably ascendant since the mid-nineteenth century, nevertheless important national differences in their histories have been significant in the dynamic development of those theoretical ideologies which inform the content of educational knowledge. The selective appropriation of knowledge in the curriculum in each country reflects the variations in the content of their hegemonic ideologies. Other interesting contrasts can be made between the ideologies of the older capitalist countries of western Europe, and Japan, on the one hand, and the new settler states like America, Canada and Australia on the other.

One of the most fascinating issues for a Marxist analysis of the formal curriculum is how and why the organization of knowledge changes. There are two distinct levels of problem here. On the one hand, the basic question of what it means to be educàted can be analysed: what specific overall organization of knowledge is considered appropriate for an educated person. On the other hand, one can examine different elements or fragments of this knowledge and trace the changes in the underlying value, political and social assumptions over time in the context of the socioeconomic framework and the course of the class struggle in different national contexts. To reiterate, there is a social basis for the transformations in the curriculum. They cannot be understood in idealist terms as simply the result of the 'growth of knowledge' or alterations in the preoccupations and perceptions of the knowledge producers. These latter themselves need to be explained.

In what follows a number of substantive cases will be examined which all involve changes in the organization and content of the curriculum in order to show the distinctiveness of a Marxist methodology for their analysis. The first illustration concerns the gradual demise in Britain of a broad humanistic curriculum based upon a study of the classics. Such a curriculum aimed to generate a world view appropriate to the life of a 'cultivated gentleman', but was gradually undermined by specialization tendencies both within the separate disciplines and within the curriculum as a whole. This process resulted in a much more fragmentary and partial approach to knowledge, with little pretence of providing a holistic analysis of society and history and the place of man within it. We have already commented upon this degeneration in the discussion of the development of bourgeois sociology since its classical founders. Gramsci writes of a similar process in Italy with the 'reforms' of the Italian education system under Mussolini. The days of an Acton, a Carlyle, a J.S. Mill or a Croce were over.

The explanation would have to lie in an account of the end of the great period of imperialist expansion, the onset of economic depression and crises from the 1890s onwards, the heightening of class struggles and the economic and social legacy of the First World War. The eighteenth and nineteenth centuries had produced in Europe the idea of progress, only explicable in terms of rapid industrialization. During the 1850s and 1860s there was a great spirit of optimism in Victorian England, coinciding with a renewed phase of expansion in the capitalist accumulation process. The Victorian era ended with a period of imperialism which masked the growing crisis in accumulation characterized by increasing concentration and centralization of capital. The growth of specialization reflects a bourgeois class in retreat into more secure territory (Plumb, 1973), the onset of pessimism and the return to the harsher objective realities which capitalism in the heyday of its expansionist phase had temporarily transcended.

Another phenomenon of the same period was the growth of the progressive education movement and the transformation of the American school system. Progressivism as institutionalized in education involved both a movement towards a more pragmatic, utilitarian and socially relevant curriculum, together with an emphasis on a child-centred pedagogy. The background to its emergence were the phenomena referred to in the previous paragraph. In a context of developing monopoly capitalism and the heightened class antagonisms which accompanied this process, a political need was generated both for an enlarged interventionist state to enhance its economic and political capacities and, furthermore, for an ideology which stressed an organic, unified society based upon class collaboration rather than class conflict. Progressive education and pragmatism involved an 'accentuation of the pragmatic subjective self as the basis for social order' (Gonzales, 1977). Given the changes in the social division of labour attendant upon the changes in monopoly capitalism, progressivism was significant ideologically as a means of adjusting people to the new economic forms in ways which did not threaten the underlying capitalist order. As Dewey wrote: 'The real question is one of reorganization of all education to meet the changed conditions of life . . . accompanying the revolution in industry. . . .' (Dewey, 1915). 'Similarly, the problem of general public school education is not to train workers for a trade but to make use of the whole environment of the child in order to supply motive and meaning to work' (p. 181).

The second set of examples concern the question of how new subjects become incorporated into the curriculum. Again it is necessary to see new curriculum developments in the context of the capital accumulation process and the changing alignment of class forces. The history of the incorporation of science into the curriculum in the nineteenth century provides an excellent illustration. As was seen in the earlier discussion of class conflicts over control and content of the schools in the period 1789-1845 the issue of science in the curriculum was seen as important by all classes contending in the political arena. Men like Paine, Owen, Richard Carlisle and the Chartists thought of it as a means of individual and social liberation, a tool for undermining mythology and the influence of religion in legitimating and masking oppressive class relations. For the bourgeoisie, on the other hand, it was seen as a vital force of production needing to be harnessed for industry and technological development. The landed classes' opposition to the introduction of science into the curriculum reflected their attempted resistance to the decline in their social hegemony consequent upon the rise of capitalism and the growth in self-confidence of a burgeoning industrial bourgeoisie. A number of writers (Cotgrove, 1958; Ashby, 1966) have provided an account of the eventual success of the bourgeoisie in institutionalizing science into the curriculum in its pure, rather than applied forms, especially in the higher reaches of the educational system. What was significant, however, was the specific mode of its incorporation and the quelling of its potentially radical implications for the working class. This occurred in such a way as to facilitate its appropriation by the bourgeois class. It became a reified body of knowledge presented as a closed system of facts or abstract theory with no overt social and political relevance. Instead of science being a medium for its emancipation, it was transformed, for the working class, into a mechanism for its domination. From it emanated ever more advanced and complicated technologies which transformed the organization of work, whilst rendering the labourer a mere instrument of machines. Similarly, the division between mental and manual labour excluded the working class from insights into scientific processes thereby depriving them of the esoteric knowledge on which the increasing control over their lives was based. Furthermore science itself increasingly elaborated theories which tended to rationalize and legitimize relations of domination and subordination. The history of psychological theories of intelligence, together with much of bourgeois sociology provide ample evidence of the appropriation of the social sciences by the bourgeoisie to serve class ends. Similarly, in spite of the major changes in the teaching of the natural sciences which have occurred in recent years, there is little evidence that the terms of the accommodation to science reached in the nineteenth century have in any way been altered. Michael Young's work on school science has simply exposed it as an ideological and value-laden activity. Science was incorporated into the framework of the hegemonic ideology in a manner which virtually excluded its radical potential (Young, 1972; Layton, 1973).

The term 'incorporation' has been used to explore the emergence of new subjects in the curriculum. Another example can be cited for the recent past: the inclusion of 'Black Studies' in the curriculum in the US. It illustrates well the dynamic aspects of the processes of maintaining hegemony. The history of Black Studies developed in the context of the growth of political organization and class consciousness among the blacks in the 1960s, reflecting the increasing economic hardship which particularly hit black communities at the end of the long post-war boom, and a work force which had always been divided along racial and ethnic lines. Although lacking a thoroughgoing theoretical analysis which would integrate race and ethnicity into a theory of class relationships, the ideology of this urban-based mass movement presented a threat in that it attacked the basis of a consensual social order based upon white domination. What happened, however, was a successful process of incorporation in which the more radical, anti-capitalist elements of the movement became isolated. An upsurge of interest in 'race relations' was generated, Black Studies courses proliferated in universities, and bourgeois scholars trebled their output of empirical studies of all aspects of black life. However, the accommodation of the black movement took place within the confines of bourgeois class relations and the theoretical resolution of the problems of blacks occurred firmly within the parameters of bourgeois social theory.

A similar situation has occurred in contemporary Australia with respect to the problems of migrants, especially those of southern European origin. In the Long Boom, Australia had relied heavily on migrant labour and had been forced to turn to southern Europe as a source of labour supplies as her traditional sources had dried up (Collins, 1975). In the 1970s migrants constituted a large proportion of the labour force engaged in manufacturing production. However, there is now a major crisis in this sector of the economy not simply because of the recession in the world economy, but because of the particular character of manufacturing production and the way in which Australia is tied into the international production and marketing system (Collins and Brezniak, 1977). Manufacturing in Australia has tended to be inefficient, protected by high tariff barriers and its expansion potential limited by the size of the local market. In the current restructuring crisis, manufacturing, and hence migrants, have been particularly badly hit as firms move their industrial production out of Australia's high-wage economy into the low-wage economies of southeast Asia. For the first time since the war, there has been developing a heightened class consciousness among, particularly, southern European sections of the migrant population and a growth of more radical forms of political organization. The response of the state has been two-fold. On the one hand, attempts have been made to curb the processes of political organization, especially through its more radical manifestations, through such actions as the dismantling of and reconstitution of 'ethnic' radio services. On the other, it is trying to initiate a major programme of incorporation by setting up elaborate consultative procedures in which leaders of the migrant communities are incorporated in the apparatuses of the state itself. One of the forms that this incorporation process takes is the encouragement of courses in multi-cultural studies designed for those who have to 'manage and deal' with migrants in the course of their professional work. Such courses are frequently premised upon a diagnosis of the problems faced by migrants in terms of a culture-clash theory. In response to migrant organization, the earlier assimilation policy has given way to an attempt to produce a pluralist, multi-cultural society in which different ethnic groups can preserve their cultural identity and way of life whilst simultaneously integrating into the dominant socioeconomic structure of white Australia. In so doing the state is attempting to head off any organization of the migrant groups which might be aimed in the long run at the capital relation (Sharp and Hartwig, 1978). The situation is further complicated by a political polarization between different ethnic communities. Migrants from southern Europe are very different economically and politically from those of Rhodesia, South Vietnam and the Baltic countries of eastern Europe.

These illustrations are necessarily sketchy, but they suffice to emphasize the need to examine innovations in the content of the curriculum historically, as the product of particular conjunctural forces which combine in their effects to require some major changes in the normal way of going about the process of education. Whilst there have been a number of studies generated by the new sociology of education into the social organization of school subjects and their underlying value and political assumptions most of them have been ahistorical and microsociological in their orientation. They lack the theoretical sensitivity of, for example, Finn, Grant and Johnson's examination of the changing social basis of the sociology of education in relationship to recent socio-historical processes. A Marxist methodology is both structural and historical. Only through a materialist study of history can the ideological content of the curriculum adequately be revealed.

Although the possibility of incorporation is always present, given the power of the dominant class through its control over the apparatuses which effect an ideological mediation, it would be wrong to define struggles over the definition of knowledge and the curriculum as politically unimportant. Even when new areas of knowledge, initially seen as threatening to hegemonic dominance, have undergone an incorporated reconstitution, this does not mean that they lose for all time their potential for pushing back the boundaries of consciousness to the point at which the basis of the capital relation becomes visible. The extent to which such a process occurs depends, of course, on the balance of class forces. Where they are fairly evenly matched, as in Italy in the 1970s, the battle for hegemony renders all areas of knowledge an open field for the class struggle. It is in such situations that the idea of the political impartiality of the scholar becomes impossible to sustain.

It is possible to see this political element in any definition of what counts as knowledge in the discipline of economics. The latter is of crucial significance given its role in legitimating bourgeois class relations and in providing technical prescriptions concerning economic policy to resolve the various problems in the accumulation process. Marx himself, of course, in *Capital, Theories of Surplus Value* and elsewhere, laid bare the ideological foundations of classical political economy, in the work of such thinkers as Adam Smith and Ricardo and their consequent failure to penetrate the commodity form and generate the theory of surplus value. Despite Marx's critique, bourgeois economics has taken a number of turns since Böhm-Bawerk, through Marshall and marginal-ism, through Keynesianism and its ultimate demise into the conflicts between monetarism and neo-Ricardianism of the 1960s and 1970s, accompanied by a resurgence of Marxian economics. None of these major shifts can be understood in isolation from the socio-historical conditions in which they are generated. The course of economic theory reproduces in ideological form the trajectory of the capitalist mode of production in its various stages and international contexts. Its history has its analogies in the earlier discussion of sociology in which a relation-ship was drawn between the attack on consensual models of the social order and their replacement by those stressing conflict and the effects of the slowing down of the third technological revolution, the onset of the current accumulation crisis and the crisis of hegemony that ensued. In the last few years the social sciences have become internally in-creasingly polarized, the political content of competing theories more apparent and the academic community of social scientists more divided internally than has been the case for a long time. In the 1970s the ideological splits within different disciplines in the metropolitan centres of capital accumulation acquire a greater visibility as the state increasingly attempts to reconstitute the basis of its hegemony. This process necessitates a growing intervention in what was once a free market place in the realm of ideas. That traditional freedom of academic enquiry, one of the king-pins of liberal democratic theory, may well suffer a long term demise and become the mythology it has always been in the periphery regions where the conditions for continued capital accumulation and the class struggle do not permit the luxury of liberal democratic forms. As Marx argued: 'bougeois right(s) never transcends the social framework in which they are articulated . . .' (Marx, 1951).

William Tyndale: a crisis in capitalism or a crisis in schooling?

In the last decade coinciding with the downturn in capital accumulation and the restructuring of capitalist production to regenerate the accumulation process, much public attention has been focused on the adequacy of schooling in meeting what are defined euphemistically as 'community needs'. A recurring target in these debates have been informal, progressive approaches to teaching and learning. These are seen as constituting an attack on the traditional role of the school as a transmittor of both the necessary skills for job performance and, more importantly, of the appropriate attitudes towards authority and order. In the midst of the debate over the Black Papers, Norman Bennett's study of informally organized schools (Bennett, 1976), and the N.F.E.R. research which seemed to show a definite downturn in reading standards which appeared to be correlated with the growth of 'progressive' pedagogy, the debate over William Tyndale threatens to become a *cause célèbre*, raising rhetorical issues of accountability and control which form the central themes in the great debate about schooling, now occurring in many western capitalist societies.

The child-centred pedagogy being practised at William Tyndale was not fundamentally the reason for the controversy. The Plowden Report had elevated progressivism into the dominant educational ideology concerning primary education (Davis and Bernstein, 1969), and many schools, especially those in inner cities were functioning along lines which for years had been regarded as good progressive educational practice. What was distinctive about Tyndale was its catchment area – in Islington which had undergone a considerable upgrading in its social class composition in the late 1950s and 1960s whilst simultaneously having the highest unemployment levels among adult males of any borough in Great Britain with the exception of Glasgow, and some of the worst conditions of housing. Thus in one school coexisted the children of wealthy, professional parents whose own class position depended on their education, and who were anxious not to deny their status to their children, the offspring of skilled working-class parents who often define education as important for their children's mobility, and a sizeable proportion of what educators define as 'socially disadvantaged pupils'. Now there is enough evidence to suggest that a child-centred methodology *per se* is not necessarily going to undermine the school's traditional role in reproducing the class structure. At Tyndale, however, the teachers were engaged in a deliberate attempt to engage in positive discrimination in favour of the 'difficult' children and their time and effort were allocated accordingly (Gretton and Jackson, 1976). Moreover, unlike many other schools, they were not prepared to channel disruptive students into special units or schools for the maladjusted. Nor, given these educational goals, was there any special stress on the need for discipline and good order. The practical ideologies and material practices which support disciplined attitudes to authority were eschewed in favour of a more relaxed and permissive pedagogy (Ellis *et al.*, 1976).

The outcome of the William Tyndale affair is well known: the managers, Local Authority and teachers battled between them. The Auld Enquiry was set up by the ILEA, the teachers eventually dismissed and the school reorganized. They had taken literally the professional slogan of teacher autonomy, were somewhat naive regarding the strength of outside pressure groups compared with the limitations on their own power. They had made little attempt to establish a social basis of support in the community (ILEA, 1966), were without any power basis in the Teachers' Union and had little liaison or linkages with any organized groups elsewhere. On the other hand, their opponents had powerful leverage outside and the advantage of operating in an environment where the crisis of capitalism was being publicly debated as a crisis of schooling. What seems clear is that William Tyndale was an example of a school which, if found more generally would undoubtedly present a threat to the prevailing hegemony. It was not performing its ideological role for the reproduction of capitalist social relations effectively, an ideological role which becomes even more salient in conditions of high unemployment. Moreover, in a context where there is both a simultaneous proletarianization of mental labour and high unemployment, especially among school leavers, a school which was obviously not even attempting to safeguard the educational privileges of its middle-class pupils was bound to become a focus of political controversy. The autonomy of the teacher seems only to be permissible where teachers' practices do not threaten the prevailing hegemony (Bailey, 1977).

What is really at the heart of the Tyndale controversy, the Black Paper debates and the controversy over 'standards' (Cox and Dyson, 1971), is the attempt to reconstitute schooling at a time of crisis in the capitalist system to effect new and superior modes of integration in a context where social order is fragile. Schools are vulnerable because the liberal view of education has always included the idea of education providing an adequate preparation for the job market, whatever other goals are espoused. Where students fail to find jobs, this tends to be interpreted by liberal educators as a failure of schooling. What is not recognized overtly is the underlying dynamics of capitalist accumulation which necessarily entails a rise in the organic composition of capital – a substitution of capital for labour – a throwing out of the labour force into unemployment. The cutback in the public service and the re-allocation of public expenditure towards the private sector of the economy is only part of the process of the restructuring of capitalist production which is occurring everywhere in the industrialized capitalist nations. It is associated with abnormally high levels of unemployment which inevitably follow the necessary drive to raise the rate of surplus value. The great debate about schooling is ideologically only a symptom of more fundamental problems, the need to reorganize the conditions for continual capital accumulation whilst simultaneously safeguarding hegemony. The school's ideological role in this process is obviously crucial. This explains the recent upsurge of interest on the part of the state in the forms and practices of schooling. This parallels its increasing role in the restructuring of capitalist work processes for which the products of schooling are being prepared.

Conclusion

In this chapter, the concepts elaborated in Chapter 4 have been applied to the analysis of schooling. The emphasis has been throughout to illustrate the way in which the historical evolution of capitalist educational systems needs to be understood against a background of the dynamics of the accumulation process and the changing patterns of class relationships. Although running the risk of overgeneralization the thesis seems plausible that in the course of the nineteenth century the ruling class gained effective control over a crucial instrument for establishing its dominance: the form and content of schooling. This process facilitated therefore, the increasing management of knowledge in the service of the technical problems generated by the accumulation process and the requirements of maintaining hegemony. The last century has seen a progressive replacement of what the Frankfurt School define as practical reason by technical reason. Education for most no longer involves the transfer of sweetness and light (Arnold, 1961), the initiation of the young into a broad and general humanistic curriculum. Even at its highest levels, the emphasis is on training pupils in those specific instrumental skills required by a differentiated work force through a range of practical ideologies which serve to reinforce and legitimize the social relations of production. The changes in the social role of the university and the threats to its always precarious autonomy illustrate the way in which specialized theoretical knowledge is appropriated to serve class ends. The demise of practical, as opposed to technical, rationality renders the task of generating a genuine counter-hegemony that much more problematic. This is because the increasing fragmentation of knowledge into narrowly focused specialisms leaves most people, outside the scope of their occupational role, subjected to the 'tyranny of common sense', a common sense structured throughout by hegemonic meanings. Even intellectual work has become bureaucratized. As Weber was only too aware, among the intelligentsia, the charisma of cultivation is replaced by a pragmatic vocationalism. However the process is a contradictory one, just as Gramsci foresaw. The trend towards the proletarianization of mental labour which mass education has partly accentuated and the increasingly precarious occupational security of many members of both the old and the new middle class create the ideological preconditions for a new counter-hegemony. There is no guarantee, however, that this counter-hegemony will be premised upon a radical analysis and critique of capitalism. It could equally be founded upon the kind of petit bourgeois, anti-monopoly, anti-working-class ideology which played such a decisive role in the development of fascism (Poulantzas, 1974). In order to fight against such a possibility, the question now arises of the relationship of theory to practice. It is to this issue that we now turn.

6 What is to be done?

It would be inappropriate in a final chapter of a study devoted to Marxism and its applicability to education simply to conclude with the customary enumeration of the various fields where further research is required. Marxism is not a closed system of thought but a set of guiding ideas and a conceptual analytic framework which, undoubtedly, raises many unanswered questions in the course of its application. With respect to all the substantive themes discussed in the previous chapter, there are many significant issues still to be resolved: areas which remain wide open for the keen research worker who might be inspired by the broad brush strokes of the analysis to dig deeper and elaborate its intricacies with a greater subtlety than has here been possible.

Marxism, however, is more than just another point of view. It is inspired by a critique of class societies, and a political commitment to work to transcend the deformations inherent in relations of domination and exploitation. More specifically, it offers an analysis of capitalism which systematically exposes the poverty of liberal theory and the essentially rhetorical nature of its moral ideals which purport to bind the system together and offer inspiration to political practice. Marxism is, as Gramsci described it: a philosophy of praxis. Whilst its insights are intellectually satisfying, they are not self-justifying. They rather serve to point the way to an alternative political practice designed to strengthen a social movement committed to overcome relations of exploitation and achieve a better future for human self-realization. This does not entail an essentialist view of human nature or of man's essence but involves recognizing that human subjects are constituted within the ensemble of social relationships which structure social intercourse, and a belief in the possibility of establishing historically specific social forms which are more conducive conditions for human freedom than those of class societies.

These assumptions generate criteria to specify in more detail those research problems which are of strategic significance to those whose social practice takes place within the formal institutions of schooling. Only three will be singled out for discussion. The judgment concerning their importance rests, of course, on a prior commitment to historical materialism. In this book, the author has tried to make out a persuasive case in its favour and criticize its main rival: liberalism. There are numerous aspects of the Marxist tradition which have not been touched upon. An assumption will be made here, that the reader has found the case convincing and has, either through prior conviction or further study, become committed to a Marxist analysis of historical change and of capitalism specifically.

The question then arises as to how to communicate those insights to others. It is not through intellectual argument and reasoning alone that people can come to realize the power of historical materialism and thus weaken capitalist hegemony. However, educators, whose social role is legitimated by the authority of their knowledge and the duty to enlighten others, cannot afford to ignore completely the place of rational argument and persuasion. Fortunately, the problem itself is amenable to rational exploration. It is concerning this issue that the theory of ideology comes into its own. Nevertheless, not nearly enough attention has been given to the question of how intellectual change can be effected in people who live their lives within ideology. This implies the necessity of further work on the ideological content of common sense, its contradictory elements and potential weak points to elucidate the positive content in the semiotics of common-sense language and other sign systems. It is a well-established insight that the task of persuading others to one's viewpoint depends upon adequately apprehending the ideological space within which the other lives. The everyday assumptions and practices which inform people's outlook need to be clarified. Only thereby can the message be tailored to gear into the positive elements of different ideological systems to achieve a theoretical rupture. One has to avoid alienating those who can be potential allies so long as the right methods are used and the appropriate cues transmitted. The history of Italian fascism illustrates this point well. Whilst there were many breaks with the past in fascist ideology, part of its power lay in the way it capitalized upon deeply felt populist, nationalist and democratic sentiments which pervaded the consciousness of the masses. Elements of subordinate classes were won to fascism from the peasantry, the old and new petit bourgeoisie and the working class: the same strata that provided the social basis of support for the socialist movement. The struggle for hegemony over such classes during this period was won by groups who reconstituted powerful elements of the existing ideology instead of superimposing an ideological message which was radical in *all* its dimensions. Progressive ideological change must generate crucial continuities. It must not neglect the positive and transcendent aspects of common-sense consciousness, even if they too are infused with hegemonic assumptions and meanings. This is precisely the lesson to be drawn from an analysis of the way the dominant ideology works. It emphasizes continuity even whilst simultaneously generating discontinuity, if the balance of class forces requires it. All subordinate classes have elements within their ideology which designate them as classes to be won from the dominant hegemony, especially in times of recession when the objective conditions are favourable, as they are now.

Second, a more precise specification of the class structure of capitalist societies is required. If the political goal is to build a mass movement in opposition to the power of capital, then thought needs be addressed to the dynamic changes occurring in the class structure, to the objective basis for the potential radicalization of different class fractions, and to the kind of issues which can be used to generate class alliances and forge lines of collective action. This is particularly important since capitalist hegemony works by fragmenting and isolating the work force and individualizing issues, thus rendering it more difficult to break free from a bourgeois world view. Of critical significance is the identification of those political questions which have the potential for overcoming the fetishized modes of thought and ideological practice characteristic of capitalism.

The field of education provides an excellent example of why this is important. The interests of the dominant classes are served by the horizontal and vertical differentiation of the workers involved in schooling. The conflicts of interest between teachers at different levels, reinforced by their fragmentation into small groups centred on numerous schools, colleges and universities, often prevent the articulation of common interests which transcend immediate and local concerns. There are, however, issues which excite a more than purely defensive reaction to offensives of the capitalist class, and which could be used to activate a political practice based upon common rather than sectional goals. Much more attention needs to be given to the identification of such issues, thereby providing a basis for uniting different groups to take the offensive and project themselves as the representatives of social rather than private interest. These questions are important theoretically, but they are absolutely vital for generating an appropriate political practice.

The third area of significance concerns the need to continue searching for the elements of our educational history, to rediscover those social movements which in their various ways tried to go beyond the constraining features of the *status quo*. Just as there is a tendency to eternize the nature of capitalism in bourgeois social theory, so educational institutions are thought of ahistorically as if they have always existed in the same form, their educational purposes unchanged and rarely questioned. Recent educational historiography, on the other hand, as has been illustrated, sheds a very different light on the course of educational change. Schooling has always been the site of conflicting social and ideological pressures, the present embodying the result of past struggles and compromises, never finally resolved and always open to new initiatives. A rediscovery and a reinterpretation of our history can throw light on this process and help to historicize the nature of contemporary schooling. It can also inspire those involved in present struggles with a sense of continuity with previous endeavours to achieve a better future, whilst enlightening about the mistakes and lessons of past practice.

What kind of political practice is thus called for from educators whose theoretical understanding of education has been influenced by Marxism? There are two distinct levels at which activity should take place: on the one hand, the practice within and about formal schooling, and on the other, a more generalized practice which goes beyond purely educational issues and takes place in a broader political arena.

It was suggested in Chapter 5 that because schools tend to reproduce capitalist social relations, it does not follow that this is inevitable or that they do so without reproducing the contradictions which characterize capitalist social formations. In their own right they are important arenas for class struggle. Indeed, given the enlarged role of the state in the accumulation process and the size of the public sector of employment, any state apparatus is a significant field for political practice. It follows from the previous discussion of the fundamental role of coercion in the maintenance of class dominance that in the last analysis, and in the long run, struggles within the repressive apparatuses of the state, the police, the military, and the legal system, will prove to be the most critical. However, the personnel of these apparatuses are themselves products of the educational system, and the ideologies within which they function are not unaffected by the wider social context and the balance of class forces therein. It would be quite wrong to define political practice within the educational system as insignificant or judge it in a patronizing way as Althusser tends to do (Althusser, 1971b). He writes:

I ask the pardon of those teachers who, in dreadful conditions, attempt to turn the few weapons they can find in the history and 'learning' they teach against the ideology, the system and the practices in which they are trapped. They are a kind of hero. But they are rare, and how many, (the majority) do not even begin to suspect the 'work' the system (which is bigger than they are and crushes them) forces them to do, or worse, put all their heart and ingenuity into performing it with the most advanced awareness (the famous new methods!). So little do they suspect it that their own devotion contributes to the maintenance and nourishment of this ideological representation of the school, which makes the school today as 'natural' indispensable – useful and even beneficial for our contemporaries as the church was 'natural', indispensable, and generous for our ancestors a few centuries ago.

Whilst some of the argument is to the point, the case is overstated (Erben and Gleeson, 1977). It suggests a determinist reproduction of the relations of production by the educational system which tends to contradict Althusser's own thesis of the relative autonomy of the ideological and political levels and lead to a form of reductionism. It also provides no hope that subjects can ever escape from ideology. Although the liberal view that education can bring about a fundamental change in the social structure is naive and whilst any *major* progressive change is unlikely, given the reality of class domination over the forms and content of schooling, this does not entail the futility of engaging in struggles to transform education. Quite the reverse. There is no one sure way to bring about a recognition of the nature of capitalism as a system, but progressive and collective struggles premised on a desire to improve education which confront structural obstacles in the form of arbitrary power can go some way to engender a greater self-awareness of what mass schooling is all about and how and through what mechanisms it is controlled. When struggles fail or do not achieve the intended goals, the possibility of retreating into either cynicism, or personalistic moralisms towards the representatives of class power encountered in the struggle, is very real. It is here that a superior analysis of how the system is constituted and where education fits in, is so important. It can also help to identify those issues which *can* be achieved in order to build up a degree of self-confidence to prepare for the next series of demands which will then be backed up by a stronger collective movement. It is completely naive to think that the really key issues can be confronted before successes have been gained on a wide variety of fronts, over what sometimes seem very trivial issues. Setbacks have to be surmounted, and an effective counter-hegemony generated which has the power of numbers behind it. The task of building a strong, united anti-capitalist movement is a long one. It may never be achieved in most of our lifetimes. Marxists have, however, a responsibility to the future. There is no necessary conflict of interests between people undergoing schooling now, and those who will be born and schooled a hundred years hence. If a historical materialist analysis of the effects of class domination in class societies generally is correct, then all political practice should be judged in terms of whether it achieves a greater awareness of those processes.

What, then, are the issues over which political practice within schools is both desirable and necessary?

The first concerns the practices and rituals which pervade schooling both in regard to teacher-pupil relationships and with respect to the even more critical relationships between educators and those who hold the power which affects them at the micro level. Whilst the constraints emanating from the system are very real, and cannot be willed away, some autonomy at the local level for schools and staff is possible. A democratization of decision-making procedure should be fought for. The hierarchical nature of decision-making within schools is difficult to justify within liberal ideology and is certainly incompatible with a broader commitment to social democracy. More importantly, its existence often presents a barrier against the implementation of progressive policies. This does not mean that such policies necessarily ensue from democratically organized schools – often quite the reverse – but without a struggle for democratization by teachers there will be little chance of gaining control over such issues as the appointment and deployment of teaching personnel, the content of the curriculum, and styles of pedagogy. Of course this 'worker participation' can only be very limited, since it involves participating in decisions, the scope of which are determined elsewhere. Moreover, there is an ever present danger of incorporation such that participation in decision-making could entail participating in the conditions of domination themselves.

Of considerable interest to radical educators is the question of the practice and rituals which structure teacher-pupil relationships. Many argue for permissiveness and freedom for the pupil, a reaction against the authoritarianism implied by traditional approaches to pedagogy. Whilst authoritarianism obviously serves the interests of capital, its reverse in libertarianism does not necessarily serve to undermine the social relationships of domination on which capitalism depends. Indeed, a pedagogical ideology of permissiveness and freedom may be particularly appropriate for capital, given certain social conditions, and do little to generate an effective counter-hegemony. It may, rather, help to reinforce the illusion that individual freedom within capitalist societies is possible without any fundamental transformation of the system (Sharp, 1976). A distinction needs to be made between authoritativeness and authoritarianism. It seems feasible to open up the relationships between teachers and taught, without simultaneously abrogating the authority of the knowledge which the teacher possesses, and the responsibility that flows from that knowledge to pupils who lack it. This does not imply that pupils should not be encouraged to participate in discussion about decisions which affect them but it does entail a view of 'pupil power' as reactionary, since it involves transferring power to those whose ideologies themselves are affected by precisely those hegemonic meanings from which they need to be weaned. This view need not conflict with the earlier discussion of the need to take account of the content of the already existing ideologies which people inhabit. What it does point to is one of the few advantages of compulsory schooling. It provides an opportunity for a systematic counter-hegemony to be presented to those whose exposure to the mass media and other ideological apparatuses is such that they may never elsewhere encounter it.

Perhaps the most critical arena for struggles within schools concerns the question of the curriculum. The growth of specialization and vocationalism, the tendency for knowledge to concern itself with the phenomenal forms of the world of appearances, the ideology of impartiality and value freedom all serve to render it difficult to penetrate the ideological content of educational knowledge and realize its emancipatory potential. The object of a progressive policy regarding the curriculum should be to create the conditions whereby a recognition of capitalism as a historically specific system with its own inner logic becomes feasible. Such a recognition may be facilitated by the breaking down of arbitrary subject barriers but this does not necessarily follow. An in-depth analysis of literature, geography or of history, informed by historical materialism, may do far more to sensitize people to the nature of the system than low-level interdisciplinary courses concerned with such problems as the ecological crisis or the poverty of the third world. Both collections and integrated knowledge codes (Bernstein, 1971) have the potential for generating counter-hegemonic meanings so long as those who teach them have made the break with bourgeois thought. However, team teaching brings teachers together in a context which gives the opportunity to those who have achieved that theoretical synthesis to engage in intellectual debate with their colleagues, thereby engendering a further potential for exposing more to the kind of analysis presented here. In many cases it is not intellectual or political opposition which provokes resistance to an anti-capitalist analysis, but simply ignorance of what such an analysis might entail.

The main goal of struggles over the curriculum is to maximize the possibility of exposing more pupils to a basic analysis of the capitalist institutions they inhabit, in a way which demonstrates the intellectual bankruptcy of liberal thought, the contradictory nature of its key assumptions, and the poverty of the solutions it offers for the social ills of our time. What specific actions concerning the curriculum are dictated will depend very much on a conjunctural analysis of the wider social forces and the specific characteristics of each school or educational institution. At one time, a purely defensive policy might be called for, at others an offensive strategy. It depends upon the balance of forces at both the macro and the micro levels.

At this juncture, some may wish to raise an objection against using the teaching situation as a context for articulating political ideals and philosophies. Such an objection depends upon the fetishized separation of education and politics in liberal theory discussed earlier. It was argued that all education is political since it entails projecting a vision of man and society which necessarily is normative, involving judgments about legitimate activity. It cannot avoid being so. A typically liberal educational practice rests on the belief that it is morally desirable to present a variety of points of view to the pupils who are then encouraged to make up their own minds. What is not recognized is the extent to which a selection has already occurred regarding which points of view are deemed worthy of consideration or the manner in which such points of view are already infected by ideological modes of apprehending reality. One's intellectual integrity is not enhanced by evading the manner in which one's own point of view influences the way the issues are presented. As Weber saw, rational debate does not demand that an intellectual or moral stance is avoided. What it does entail is that the stance adopted is itself open to rational scrutiny, the basic assumptions exposed for critical appraisal and the sequences in the discourse examined for their logical consistency. It is important that all teachers, regardless of their political opinions, should explain what their own views are and be prepared to have them subjected by the pupils to critical scrutiny. Historical materialism has little to fear in this respect. Precisely because it is a superior mode of analysis, it can withstand rational appraisal and be confident when juxtaposed with other systems of thought.

Leaving pupils to make up their own minds before they have been exposed to the full range of relevant arguments is a retreat from reason. It may, of course, be the case that teachers themselves have not decided what they believe. However, having the courage to admit that there are issues which are not fully understood, is the first step towards a genuine educative relationship.

Above all, it is important to try to convey the possibility of alternatives. One of the strongest ideological supports for capitalism is the way it has generated a belief in its own necessity even among those who are its strongest critics. There are, however, a variety of ways in which the belief in its necessity and timelessness can be undermined. Such disciplines as history, anthropology and even the classics and literature have a role to play here.

But, more cogently, even within capitalist societies themselves there are moments of transcendence which, whilst often reflecting capitalist societies' contradictions, point to the possibility of moving beyond them; in literature, art and music, in love and friendship and in the spontaneity, free from ideology, of very young children. The fact that great works of art can be widely appreciated demonstrates the possibility of universal truths which gear into the positive aspects of common sense consciousness. Again, however, the problem of the means by which such a message can be communicated looms large.

Finally, it is important not to expect or to hope for too much. Schooling in capitalist society is capitalist schooling: there will be many who, for a variety of reasons, will turn away from a counter-hegemony. The power which resides in the dominant ideology to incorporate radical initiatives is very pervasive and has to be fought against continu-ally. The tendency to personalize failure has to be counteracted through fostering peer-group support to withstand the frustrations of operating within schools which are ultimately under capitalist control. Of course, the successes are not due to individual effort and will alone, although (with no apologies to Althusser) such concepts do have their place within a Marxist political practice. The broader parameters of the class struggle in the context of the accumulation process impinge upon the educator's actions and frustrate or reward his exertions. It is the articu-lation of collective will with the objective conditions which will influ-ence the outcome of any specific counter-hegemonic practice.

It would be inconsistent with our general thesis regarding the per-vasiveness of bourgeois ideology in capitalist societies, to limit the discussion of praxis to the specific context of schooling. The mere existence of full-time educational institutions and professional educators legitimates the distinction between mental and manual labour which it is part of a socialist strategy to overcome. The struggle for hegemony takes place beyond the school as well as within it and needs to be engaged in at every level where hegemonic meanings penetrate: in such contexts as the family, the trade union, community organizations, political parties at state and local level, and the media. It is important that socialist teachers do not become isolated from other social move-ments because in the last analysis, it is only through a strong mass movement that class domination can be transcended. The obstacles against building such a mass movement should not be underestimated. As Gramsci recognized, many of the organizations articulating the demands of subordinate classes developed out of the need to organize defensively against the initiatives of the bourgeois class. Consequently, both their organizational form and political programs reflect the 'impress' of the capitalist class and they are therefore incapable of generating an anti-capitalist strategy. Trade unions, for example, with few exceptions, tend to be oligarchic in their structure, their leadership isolated from their mass base, and incorporated both ideologically and institutionally with the apparatuses of the social democratic state. They articulate economistic policies and their strategy is narrowly defensive and sectional whereas what is urgently needed is a platform which can articulate the needs of social labour as a whole. Similarly, those political parties which claim to represent the interests of sub-ordinate classes tend to be reformist and elitist and do little to foster a counter-hegemonic vision. Although struggles within such institutions are necessary since they do have roots in the masses, there is an urgent need to search for new organizational forms independent from capitalist control in which mass-based initiatives can be taken up and organized. The criterion for action within traditional class-based organizations like trade unions and political parties and within new organizational forms should be whether the issues being raised work to generate a broader understanding of the nature of capitalist societies and foster unity rather than dissension among all those groups subjected to the power of capital. It is essential to encourage a class analysis of the issues being debated, whether they concern housing or medical services, technological or youth unemployment, the ecological 'crisis', racism or sexism. Without such a class analysis, there is a danger that other more reactionary initiatives may capture the middle ground of social democratic politics, especially in a context of a growing vacuum at the centre engendered by economic recession and political and ideological forces. Such problems are not irrelevant either in the short or the long term to the enlightened educator. Their solution depends upon the creation of organic intellectuals within the subordinate strata of the calibre of those leaders of the working class in the nineteenth century who saw so clearly that the main obstacle in the way of a liberated future for everyone was the capitalist system and were sceptical of the possibilities of its regeneration. Above all, the class character of the ideology of social democracy and its intrusion into the working class via Fabianism and trade unionism has to be exposed. This can only be achieved by penetrating into the centre of capitalism's logic, the profit motive, and demonstrating the class nature of the state and its illusory autonomy.

This book is being written at a time of world economic recession in which a major restructuring of capitalist production is taking place to regenerate the conditions for expanded reproduction (Fine, 1975). A restructuring process has economic, political and ideological dimensions, each of which have significant implications for the basic relationship between capital and labour. However, whilst restructuring itself cannot be prevented so long as the capitalist system persists, its forms are not predetermined. A variety of options are possible and which ones are chosen will depend very much on the balance of political and ideological forces. It is vital that those strata affected do not adopt a merely short term, defensive and sectional reaction to the processes involved, but actively participate in a movement to ensure that the terms of the eventual accommodation enhance the possibility for further mass mobilization and do not impede it. For example, the current attempts to restructure capitalist educational systems to reconstitute hegemony are a legitimate object of political practice. The form of its restructuring could be reactionary or progressive. It will only be the latter if a collective mass struggle is engaged in to prevent a reactionary and demobilizing outcome. The bourgeois class and its executive committee in the state must not be left to make the running; for if it does so, the conditions for renewed struggle are rendered more problematic.

Conclusion

The author makes no apologies for the plea for commitment implied in this chapter. Although it has not been possible to spell out in detail the arguments as to how and why capitalism is a system based upon class domination and incapable of fulfilling its promises either nationally, or more pertinently, on a world scale, the evidence for its failure is apparent for all with the will to see. It follows from a Marxist explanation of why this is so that one should be morally and politically committed to work for its demise. An organization of production based upon the satisfaction of human needs would be infinitely superior to one in which production is carried on for exchange. Given private appropriation, the latter means, essentially, production for capitalist profit, only possible through the artificial generation of needs to satisfy the imperative of accumulation. As Marx wittily put it, 'Accumulate, accumulate, that is Moses and the prophets' (Marx, 1974a, vol. 1, p. 595).

Nevertheless, it would be foolish not to recognize the obvious dangers in a political strategy such as the one advocated here. To the extent that it is succeeding, those bourgeois rights and freedoms that have served capitalism so well, at least in the metropolitan centres of capital accumulation (although not elsewhere, or even there when capitalist hegemony seemed vulnerable) may eventually become superfluous. Bourgeois educational systems have proudly legitimated their autonomy from politics through their commitment to academic freedom: the freedom to think, to enquire, to communicate, to publish. They have boasted their superiority over the educational systems of eastern Europe which undoubtedly serve the interests of those oppressive bureaucratic state capitalist regimes which have rendered Marxism, unwarrantedly, a dirty word in many quarters. However, the differences between the two systems in terms of their commitment to formal rights, are gradually being eroded. More than anything at the present conjuncture, it is necessary to struggle to preserve those rights, to fight against a resurgence of intellectual McCarthyism which can so stifle criticism and demobilize opposition, thus rendering the belief in the emancipatory potential of education nothing but the hollow rhetoric it has always been for so many.

It is appropriate to conclude with a quotation from Gramsci:

we must have done with the inconclusive whinings of the eternally innocent. Every man must be asked to account for the manner in which he has fulfilled the task that life has set him and continue to set him day by day; he must be asked to account for what he has done, but especially for what he has not done.

It is high time that the social chain should not weigh on just the few; it is time that events should be seen to be the intelligent work of men, and not the products of chance, of fatality. And so it is time to have done with the indifferent among us, the sceptics, the people who profit from the small good procured by the activity of a few, but who refuse to take responsibility for the great evil that is allowed to develop and come to pass because of their absence from the struggle. (Gramsci, 1977, p. 18)

Bibliography

Adlam, D., *et al*. (1977), 'Psychology, ideology and the human subject', *Ideology and Consciousness*, no. 1.

Adorno, T. (1967), *Prisms*, London, Spearman.

Ahier, J. (1977), 'Philosophers, sociologists and knowledge in education', in M. Young and J. Whitty (eds), *Society, State and Schooling*, Ringmer, Falmer Press.

Althusser, L. (1968), 'La philosophie comme arme de la révolution', in *La Pensée*, no. 138, March–April.

Althusser, L. (1971a), 'Freud and Lacan', in *Lenin and Philosophy*, London, New Left Books.

Althusser, L. (1971b), 'Ideology and ideological state apparatuses', in *Lenin and Philosophy*, London, New Left Books.

Althusser, L. and Balibar, E. (1970), *Reading Capital*, London, New Left Books.

Anderson, P. (1976b), *Lineages of the Absolutist State*, London, New Left Books.

Anderson, P. (1976a), *Passages from Antiquity to Feudalism*, London, New Left Books.

Anderson, P. (1977), 'The antinomies of Antonio Gramsci', *New Left Review*, 100.

Arnold, M. (1961), *Culture and Anarchy*, Cambridge University Press.

Ashby, E. (1966), *Technology and the Academics: An Essay on Universities and the Scientific Revolution*, London, Macmillan.

Bailey, D. (1977), 'Missing out on the middle classes', *Radical Education*, 8.

Banaji, J. (1977), 'Modes of production in a materialist conception of history', *Capital and Class*, vol. 1, no. 3.

Banks, O. (1974), 'The new sociology of education: some dangers of the approach', *Forum,* Autumn.

Barthes, R. (1967), *Elements of Semiology*, London, Cape.

Barthes, R. (1972), *Mythologies*, London, Cape.

Baudelet, C. and Establet, R. (1971), *L'Ecole Capitaliste en France*, Paris, Maspero.

Bell, D. (1960), *The End of Ideology*, Glencoe, Illinois, Free Press.

Bellack, A., *et al.* (1966), *The Language of the Classroom*, New York, Teachers College Press.

Bellamy, E. (1888), *Looking Backwards. 2000-1887*, Boston, Ticknor.

Bennett, N. (1976), *Teaching Styles and Pupil Progress*, Cambridge, Mass., Harvard University Press.

Benton, T. (1974), 'Education and politics', in D. Holly (ed.), *Education or Domination*, Arrow.

Berkoff, S. (1976), *East and Other Plays*, London, J. Calder.

Bernbaum, G. (1977), *Knowledge and Ideology in the Sociology of Education*, London, Macmillan.

Bernstein, B. (1969), 'A critique of the concept of compensatory education', in *Class Codes and Control*, vol. 2, London, Routledge & Kegan Paul, 1973.

Bernstein, B. (1971a), 'On the classification and framing of educational knowledge', in M.F.D. Young (ed.), *Knowledge and Control*, London, Collier Macmillan.

Bernstein, B. (1971b), 'A sociolinguistic approach to socialization, with some reference to educability', in D. Hymes and J.V. Gumperz, *Directions in Sociolinguistics*, New York, Rinehart & Winston.

Bernstein, B. (1973), 'Social class language and socialization', in *Class Codes and Control*, vol. 2, London, Routledge & Kegan Paul.

Bernstein, B. (1975, 1977), *Class Codes and Control*, vol. 3, *Towards a Theory of Educational Transmission*, London, Routledge & Kegan Paul.

Böhm-Bawerk, E. (1975), *Karl Marx and the Close of His System*, London, Merlin Press.

Bourdieu, P. (1962), *The Algerians*, Boston, Beacon Press.

Bourdieu, P. (1971a), 'Intellectual field and creative project', in M.F.D. Young (ed.) (1971).

Bourdieu, P. (1971b), 'Systems of education and systems of thought', in M.F.D. Young (ed.) (1971).

Bourdieu, P. (1973), 'Cultural reproduction and social reproduction', in R. Brown (ed.), *Knowledge, Education and Cultural Change*, London, Tavistock.

Bourdieu, P. (1977), 'Symbolic power', in D. Gleeson, *Identity and Structure. Issues in the Sociology of Education*, Driffield, Nafferton Books.

Bourdieu, P. and Passeron, J.C. (1977), *Reproduction in Education, Society and Culture*, London, Sage.

Bowles, S. and Gintis, H. (1976), *Schooling in Capitalist America*, London, Routledge & Kegan Paul.

Braverman, H. (1974), *Labour and Monopoly Capital*, New York, Monthly Review Press.

Brennan, T. (1978), 'The class position of Marxist academics', *Intervention*, 10.

Brenner, R. (1977), 'The Origins of Capitalist Development: a Critique of Neo-Smithian Marxism', *New Left Review*, 104.

Carchedi, G. (1977), *On the Economic Identification of Social Classes*, London, Routledge & Kegan Paul.

Clarke, J., *et al.* (1976), 'Subcultures, cultures and class: a theoretical Overview', in S. Hall and T. Jefferson (eds), *Resistance and Rituals. Youth Cultures in Post War Britain*, London, Hutchinson and Birmingham Centre for Cultural Studies.

Clarke, S. (1977), 'Marxism, sociology and Poulantzas' theory of the state', *Capital and Class*, Summer.

Collins, J. (1975), 'The political economy of post war immigration', in E. Wheelwright and K. Buckley (eds), *Political Economy of Australian Capitalism*, vol. 1, A.N.Z. Press.

Collins, J. and Brezniak, M. (1977), 'The Australian crisis from boom to bust', *Journal of Australian Political Economy*, no. 1, October.

Connell, R. (1977), 'Macquarie University Study Guide on Art and Ideology', Mimeo.

Cotgrove, S. (1958), *Technical Education and Social Change*, London, Ruskin House.

Coulthard, M. (1969), 'A discussion of restricted and elaborated codes', *Educational Review*, vol. 22, no. 1.

Coward, R. (1977), 'Class culture and the social formation', in *Screen*, vol. 18, no. 1, Spring.

Coward, R. and Ellis, J. (1977), *Language and Materialism*, London, Routledge & Kegan Paul.

Cox, C. and Dyson, A. (1971), *The Black Papers on Education*, London, Davis-Poynter.

Curtius, E. (1932), *Deutscher Geist in Gefahr*, Stuttgart, Deutsche Verlagsanstalt.

Dale, R. (1977), 'Implications of the rediscovery of the hidden curriculum for the sociology of teaching', in D. Gleeson (ed.), *Identity and Structure: Issues in the Sociology of Education*, Driffield, Nafferton Books.

Davies, B. (1976), *Social Control and Education*, London, Methuen.

Davies, B. and Bernstein, B. (1969), 'Some sociological comments on Plowden', in R.S. Peters (ed.), *Perspectives on Plowden*, London, Routledge & Kegan Paul.

Davies, I. (1971), 'The management of knowledge', in M.F.D. Young (ed.) (1971).

Davis, K. and Moore, K. (1966), 'Some principles of stratification', in S.M. Lipset and R. Bendix (eds), *Class Status and Power*, New York, Free Press.

Demaine, J. (1977), 'The new sociology of education', *Economy and Society*, vol. 6, no. 2.

Dewey, J. and E. (1915), *Schools of Tomorrow*, New York, Dutton.

Dorfman, J. (1966), *Thorstein Veblen and his America*, New York, A.M. Kelley.

Dreeben, R. (1977), 'The contribution of schooling to the learning of norms', in J. Karabel and A.H. Halsey (eds), *Power and Ideology in Education*, Oxford University Press.

Durkheim, E. (1897), 'Review of Labiola Antonio's Essais sur la conception matérialiste de l'histoire', *Revue Philosophique*, XLIV.

Durkheim, E. (1905), 'Sur la séparation des églises et de l'état', in *Libres Entretiens*. 1st series, *Sur l'Internationalisme Libres Entretiens*, 2nd series.

Durkheim, E. (1947), *The Division of Labour in Society*, Chicago Free Press.

Durkheim, E. (1956), *Education and Sociology*, Chicago Free Press.

Durkheim, E. (1957), *Professional Ethics and Civil Morals*, London, Routledge & Kegan Paul.

Durkheim, E. (1961a), *The Elementary Forms of the Religious Life*, New York, Collier Books.

Durkheim, E. (1961b), *Moral Education*, New York, Free Press.

Durkheim, E. (1976), *The Evolution of Educational Theory in France*, London, Routledge & Kegan Paul.

Durkheim, E. and Mauss, M. (1963), *Primitive Classifications*, London, Cohen & West.

Eagleton, T. (1976), 'Criticism and politics: the work of Raymond Williams', *New Left Review*.

Eggleston, J. (1977), *The Sociology of the School Curriculum*, London, Routledge & Kegan Paul.

Eliot, T.S. (1963), *Notes Towards a Definition of Culture*, London, Faber & Faber.

Bibliography

Ellis, T., *et al.* (1976), *William Tyndale: the Teachers Story*, London, Writers and Readers Publishing Co-operative.

Engels, F. (1890), 'Letter to Bloch', in *Karl Marx and Frederick Engels Selected Correspondence*, Moscow, Foreign Languages Publishing House.

Erben, M. and Gleeson, D. (1977), 'Education as reproduction. A critical examination of some aspects of the work of Louis Althusser', in M. Young and J. Whitty (eds), *Society, State and Schooling*, London, Falmer Press.

Esland, G. (1971), 'Teaching and learning as the organization of knowledge', in M.F.D. Young (1971).

Fine, B. (1975), *Marx's 'Capital'*, London, Macmillan.

Finn, O., *et al.* (1977), 'Social democracy, education and the crisis', in Working Papers in Cultural Studies, 10, *On Ideology*, Birmingham, C.C.C.S.

Floud, J. (1969), 'Karl Mannheim', in T. Raison (ed.), *The Founding Fathers of Social Science. A Series from New Society*, Harmondsworth, Penguin.

Flude, M. and Ahier, J. (1974), *Educability, Schools and Ideology*, London, Croom Helm.

Freedman, N. (1967), 'Cultural deprivation: a commentary in the sociology of knowledge', *Journal of Educational Thought*, vol. 1, no. 1.

Giddens, A. (1974), *Politics and Sociology in the Thought of Max Weber*, London, Macmillan.

Gintis, H. (1972), 'Towards a political economy of education: a radical critique of Ivan Illich's reschooling society', in Ian Lister (ed.), *Deschooling*, Cambridge University Press.

Gonzales, G. (1977), 'The relationship between monopoly capitalism and progressive education', in *The Insurgent Sociologist*, vol. 7, no. 4, Fall.

Gorbutt, D. (1972), 'The new sociology of education', *Education for Teaching*, 89, Autumn.

Gouldner, A. (1970), *The Coming Crisis in Western Sociology*, New York, Basic Books.

Gouldner, A. (1973), 'Anti-minotaur. The myth of a value free sociology', in A. Gouldner, *For Sociology. Renewal and Critique in Sociology Today*, London, Allen Lane.

Gouldner, A. (1959), Introduction to E. Durkheim, *Socialism and Saint Simon*, London, Routledge & Kegan Paul.

Gramsci, A. (1971), *Selections from the Prison Notebooks*, London, Lawrence & Wishart.

Gramsci, A. (1977), 'Indifference', in *Selections from Political Writings 1910-1920*, London, Lawrence & Wishart.

Gretton, J. and Jackson, M. (1976), *William Tyndale. Challenge of a School - or a System*, London, Allen & Unwin.

Habermas, J. (1970), 'On systematically distorted communication. Towards a theory of communicative competence', *Inquiry*, no. 13.

Habermas, J. (1975), *Legitimation Crisis*, Introduction by T. McCarthy, Boston, Beacon Press.

Hall, S. (1977a) 'Culture media and the ideological effect', in J. Curran *et al.*, (eds), *Mass Communications and Society*, London, Edward Arnold and the Open University.

Hall, S. (1977b), 'The Hinterland of science: ideology and "the sociology of knowledge" ', in Working Papers in Cultural Studies, 10, *On Ideology*, Birmingham, C.C.C.S.

Hall, S., *et al.* (1977), 'Politics and ideology', in Working Papers in Cultural Studies, 10, *On Ideology*, Birmingham, C.C.C.S.

Hall, S. and Jefferson, T. (1976), *Resistance Through Rituals*, London, Hutchinson and Centre for Cultural Studies.

Hargreaves, D. (1967), *Social Relations in a Secondary School*, London, Routledge & Kegan Paul.

Harrison, J.F.C. (1961), *Learning and Living. 1790-1970*, London, Routledge & Kegan Paul.

Harrison, J.F.C. (1968), *Utopianism and Education: Robert Owen and the Owenites*, New York, Teachers College Press.

Hayward, J. (1959), 'Solidarist syndicalism: Durkheim and Deguit', *Sociological Review*, 8.

Heath, S. (1972), *The Nouveau Roman. A Study in the Practice of Writing*, London, Elek.

Hextall, I. and Sarup, M. (1977), 'School knowledge, evaluation and alienation', in M. Young and G. Whitty (eds), *Society, State and Schooling*, London, Falmer Press.

Hirst, P.Q. (1976), *Social Evolution and Sociological Categories*, London, Allen & Unwin.

Holloway, J. and Picciotto, S. (1978), *State and Capital. A Marxist Debate*, London, Arnold.

Hughes, S. (1959), *Consciousness and Society: The Reorientation of European Social Thought 1890-1930*, London, MacGibbon & Kee.

Hussein, A. (1976), 'The economy and the educational system in capitalist societies', *Economy and Society*, vol. 5, no. 4, November.

Illich, I. (1973), *Deschooling Society*, Harmondsworth, Penguin.

Inglis, F. (1975), 'The hordes of the Philistines; British sociology today', *Education for Teaching*, no. 98, Autumn.

ILEA (1976), *William Tyndale Junior and Infants School Public Inquiry* (Auld Report), I.L.E.A.

Jacka, E. (1977), 'Contributions to the Theory of Ideology', Ph.D. Thesis, University of Sydney, unpublished.

Jackson, L. (1974), 'The myth of an elaborated code', *Higher Education Review*, vol. 6, no. 2.

Jackson, P. (1968), *Life in Classrooms*, New York, Holt, Rinehart & Winston.

Jenks, C. (1976), *Rationality, Education and the Social Organization of Knowledge*, London, Routledge & Kegan Paul.

Johnson, R. (1970), 'Educational policy and social control in early Victorian England', in *Past and Present*, 49.

Johnson, R. (1976), 'Notes on the schooling of the English working classes', in R. Dale *et al.* (eds), *Schooling and Capitalism*, London, Routledge & Kegan Paul.

Johnson, R. (1976-7), 'Really useful knowledge', Part I, Part II, *Radical Education*, 7, 8.

Karabel, J. and A.H. Halsey (1977), *Power and Ideology in Education*, Oxford University Press.

Keddie, N. (1971), 'Classroom knowledge', in M.F.D. Young (ed.), *Knowledge and Control*.

Keddie, N. (ed.) (1973), *Tinker Tailor: The Myth of Cultural Deprivation*, Harmondsworth, Penguin Education.

Kennet, J. (1973), 'The sociology of Pierre Bourdieu', *Educational Review*, vol. 25, no. 3.

Kristeva, J. (1976), 'Signifying practice and mode of production', *Edinburgh Magazine*, no. 1.

Labov, W. (1973), 'The logic of non standard English', In N. Keddie (ed.), *Tinker Tailor*, Harmondsworth, Penguin.

Lacan, J. (1968), *The Language of the Self*, New York, Dell.

Lacan, J. (1970), 'The insistence of the letter in the unconscious', in J. Ehrmann (ed.), *Structuralism*, New York, Anchor.

Lacey, C. (1970), *Hightown Grammar*, Manchester University Press.

Layton, D. (1973), *Science for the People*, London, Allen & Unwin.

178

Lévi-Strauss, C. (1966), *The Savage Mind*, London, Weidenfeld & Nicolson.

Lévi-Strauss, C. (1973), *Structural Anthropology*, New York, Basic Books.

Lewis, J. (1975), *Max Weber and Value Free Sociology: A Marxist Critique*. London, Lawrence & Wishart.

Lukes, S. (1973), *Emile Durkheim: His Life and Work*, London, Allen Lane.

Luxemburg, R. (1951), *The Accumulation of Capital*, London, Routledge & Kegan Paul.

Macpherson, C.B. (1961), 'Market concepts in political theory', *Canadian Journal of Economics and Political Science*, vol. 27.

Macpherson, C.B. (1962), *The Political Theory of Possessive Individualism: Hobbes to Locke*, Oxford, Clarendon Press.

Macpherson, C.B. (1973), *Democratic Theory: Essays in Retrieval*, Oxford, Clarendon Press.

Mandel, E. (1968), *Marxist Economic Theory*, London, Merlin Press.

Mandel, E. (1975), *Late Capitalism*, London, New Left Books.

Mannheim, K. (1940), *Man and Society in an Age of Reconstruction*, London, Routledge & Kegan Paul.

Mannheim, K. (1943), *Diagnosis of Our Time*, London, Routledge & Kegan Paul.

Mannheim, K. (1951a), *Essays in the Sociology of Knowledge*, London, Routledge & Kegan Paul.

Mannheim, K. (1953), *Essays on Sociology and Social Psychology*, London, Routledge & Kegan Paul.

Mannheim, K. (1951b), *Freedom, Power and Democratic Planning*, London, Routledge & Kegan Paul.

Mannheim, K. (1952) 'Conservative thought', in *Essays on the Sociology of Knowledge*, London, Routledge & Kegan Paul.

Mannheim, K. (1960), *Ideology and Utopia*, London, Routledge & Kegan Paul.

Mannheim, K. and Stewart, W. (1962), *The Sociology of Education*, London, Routledge & Kegan Paul.

Marcuse, H. (1968), 'Industrialism and capitalism in the work of Max Weber', in *Negations*, London, Allen Lane.

Marx, K. (1970), *A Contribution to the Critique of Political Economy*, Moscow, Progress Publishers.

Marx, K. (1973a), 'Eighteenth Brumaire of Louis Bonaparte', in *Surveys from Exile*, vol. 1, Harmondsworth, Pelican.

Marx, K. (1973b), 'The class struggles in France 1848–1850', in
    Surveys from Exile, vol. 2, Harmondsworth, Pelican.
Marx, K. (1974a), *Capital*, 3 vols, London, Lawrence & Wishart.
Marx, K. (1951), 'Critique of the Gotha Programme', in Marx and
    Engels, *Selected Works*, vol. 2, Moscow, Foreign Languages
    Publishing House.
Marx, K. (1976), *Theses on Feuerbach*, in *Marx and Engels:
    Collected Works*, vol. 5, London, Lawrence & Wishart.
Marx, K. and Engels, F. (1976), *The German Ideology*, in *Marx and
    Engels: Collected Works*, vol. 5, London, Lawrence & Wishart.
Mayer, J. (1956), *Max Weber and German Politics*, London.
Mepham, J. (1973), 'The theory of ideology in capital', *Radical
    Philosophy*, 6.
Merleau-Ponty, M. (1969), *Humanism and Terror*, New York,
    Beacon Books.
Mills, C. Wright (1953), Introduction to T. Veblen (1970).
Mills, C. Wright (1959), *The Sociological Imagination*, New York,
    Oxford University Press.
Mitchell, J. (1974), *Psychoanalysis and Feminism*, London, Allen Lane.
Mommsen, W. (1959), *Max Weber und die deutsche Politique*,
    Tuebingen, J.C.B. Mohr.
Mommsen, W. (1974), *The Age of Bureaucracy: Perspective on the
    Political Sociology of Max Weber*, Oxford, Blackwell.
Murdoch, G. (1974), 'The Politics of Culture', in D. Holly (ed.),
    Education or Domination, London, Arrow.
Musgrave, P.W. (1973), *Knowledge, Curriculum and Change*, London,
    Angus & Robertson.
Nairn, T. (1977), *The Breakup of Britain*, New Left Books.
Nietzsche, F. (1909), *On the Future of our Educational Institutions;
    Homer and Classical Philology*, Edinburgh and London, T.N. Foulis.
Nisbet, R. (1967), *The Sociological Tradition*, London Heinemann.
Owen, R. and Sutcliffe, B. (1972), *Studies in the Theory of
    Imperialism*, London, Longmans.
Oxaal, I., *et al.* (1975), *Beyond the Sociology of Development*,
    London, Routledge & Kegan Paul.
Plumb, J.H. (1973), Introduction to *The Dutch Seaborne Empire
    1600–1800*, by C.R. Boxer, Harmondsworth, Pelican.
Postman, N. and Weingarten, C. (1971), *Teaching as a Subversive
    Activity*, Harmondsworth, Penguin.
Poulantzas, N. (1974), *Fascism and Dictatorship*, London, New Left
    Books.

Poulantzas, N. (1975a), *Classes in Contemporary Capitalism*, London, New Left Books.

Poulantzas, N. (1975b), *Political Power and Social Classes*, London, New Left Books.

Reimer, E. (1971), *School is Dead: An Essay on Alternatives in Education*, Harmondsworth, Penguin.

Remmling, G. (1975), *The Sociology of Karl Mannheim*, London, Routledge & Kegan Paul.

Riessman, F. (1962), *The Culturally Deprived Child*, New York, Harper & Row.

Rosen, H. (1972), *Language and Class: A Critical Look at the Theories of Basil Bernstein*, Bristol, Falling Wall Press.

Saussure, F. de (1974), *Course in General Linguistics*, London, Fontana.

Schutz, A. (1943), 'The problem of rationality in the social world', *Economica*, 10.

Seeley, J. (1966), 'The "Making" and "Taking" of problems', *Social Problems*, 14.

Shapin, S. and Barnes, B. (1977), 'Science, nature and control: interpreting Mechanics Institutes', *Social Studies of Science*, vol. 7, no. 1, February.

Sharp, R. (1976), 'Open schools, open society', *Radical Education Dossier*, no. 1.

Sharp, R. and Green, A. (1975), *Education and Social Control*, London, Routledge & Kegan Paul.

Sharp, R. and Hartwig, M. (1978), 'Multi-Cultural Studies. A Critique of Academic Senate's Working Party Report on Ethnic Studies at Macquarie University', Sidney, mimeo.

Silver, H. (1965), *The Concept of Popular Education*, London, Methuen.

Simon, B. (1960), *Studies in the History of Education 1780–1870*, London, Lawrence & Wishart.

Simon, B. (ed.), (1972), *The Radical Tradition in Education in Britain*, London, Lawrence & Wishart.

Simon, J. (1974), 'New direction sociology and comprehensive schooling', *Forum*, Autumn.

Sinclair, J.M. and Coulthard, R.M. (1975), *Towards an Analysis of Discourse*, London, Oxford University Press.

Sinha, C. (1977), 'Class language and education', *Ideology and Consciousness*, vol. 1, no. 1.

Sparks, C. (1977), 'The evolution of cultural studies', *Screen Education*, no. 22, Spring.

Stedman Jones, G. (1976), 'From historical sociology to theoretic history', *British Journal of Sociology*, vol. 27, no. 3.

Stevens, P. (1978), 'The struggle against capitalist education', *Radical Education Dossier*, vol. 5, February.

Stubbs, M. (1976), *Language, Schools and Classrooms*, London, Methuen.

Thompson, E.P. (1965), *The Making of the English Working Class*, London, Gollancz.

Timpanaro, S. (1975), *On Materialism*, London, New Left Books.

Tolson, A. (1976), 'On the semiotics of working class speech', in *Working Papers in Cultural Studies 9*. Birmingham, C.C.C.S.

Veblen, T. (1935), *The Theory of Business Enterprise*, New York, C. Scribner's Sons.

Veblen, T. (1964), *Imperial Germany and the Industrial Revolution*, New York, A.M. Kelly.

Veblen, T. (1965), *The Engineers and the Price System*, New York. A.M. Kelly.

Veblen, T. (1969), *The Higher Learning in America*, New York, Hill & Wang.

Veblen, T. (1970), *The Theory of the Leisured Class*, London, Unwin Books.

Volosinov, V.N. (1973), *Marxism and the Philosophy of Language*, London, Seminar Press.

Weber, Marianne (1975), *Max Weber: A Biography*, New York, Wiley.

Weber, M. (1946a) 'The Chinese literati', in H. Gerth and C.W. Mills (eds), *From Max Weber. Essays in Sociology*, New York, Oxford University Press.

Weber, M. (1946b) 'Bureaucracy', in H. Gerth and C.W. Mills (eds), *From Max Weber: Essays in Sociology*, New York, Oxford University Press.

Weber, M. (1949), *Methodology of the Social Sciences*, Chicago, Free Press.

Weber, M. (1964), *The Theory of Social and Political Organization*, New York, Free Press.

Weber, M. (1967), *The Protestant Ethic and the Spirit of Capitalism*, London, Unwin University Books.

Weber, M. (1968), *Max Weber on Charisma and Institutions Building*, ed. S.N. Eisenstadt, University of Chicago Press.

Weber, M. (1974), *Max Weber on Universities: The Power of the State and the Dignity of the Academic Calling in Imperial Germany*, University of Chicago Press.

White, D. (1977), 'Relationships between Schooling and Unemployment', Unpublished paper given at the Melbourne Political Economy Conference, August, 1977.

Williams, R. (1973), 'Base and superstructure in Marxist cultural theory', *New Left Review*, no. 82.

Williams, R. (1974), *Television, Technology and Cultural Form*, London, Fontana.

Williams, R. (1976), *Keywords*, New York, Oxford University Press.

Williams, R. (1977a), Book Review of *Reproduction*, in *New Society*, 5 May.

Williams, R. (1977b), *Marxism and Literature*, Oxford University Press.

Willis, P. (1976), 'The class significance of school counter culture', in M. Hammersley and P. Woods (eds), *The Process of Schooling*, London, Routledge & Kegan Paul and Open University Books.

Willis, P. (1978), *Learning to Labour*, Saxon House.

Woolf, K., ed. (1978), *From Karl Mannheim*, New York, Oxford University Press.

Woolfson, C. (1976), 'The semiotics of working class speech', in *Working Papers in Cultural Studies 9*, Birmingham, C.C.C.S.

Wright, E.O. (1976), 'Class boundaries in advanced capitalist societies', *New Left Review*, no. 98.

Young, M.F.D. (1971a), 'An approach to the curricula as socially organized knowledge', in M.F.D. Young (ed.) (1971).

Young, M.F.D. (ed.) (1971b), *Knowledge and Control*, London, Collier Macmillan.

Young, M.F.D. (1972), 'On the politics of educational knowledge', *Economy and Society*, vol. 1, no. 2.

Young, M.F.D. (1973a), 'Educational theorizing. A radical alternative', *Education for Teaching*, Summer.

Young, M.F.D. (1973b), 'Taking sides against the probable', *Educational Review*, vol. 2, no. 3, June.

Young, M.F.D. (1975a), 'Curriculum change: limits and possibilities', *Educational Studies*, vol. 1.

Young, M.F.D. (1975b), 'Sociologists and the politics of comprehensive schooling', *Forum*.

Young, M. (1975c), 'The Sociology of Knowledge: a Dialogue between John White and Michael Young', in *Education for Teaching*, no. 97.

Young, M., *et al.* (1976), *Worlds Apart: A Reader for a Sociology of Education*, London, Collier Macmillan.

Young, M. and G. Whitty (1977a), Introduction to *Explorations in the Politics of School Knowledge*, Driffield, Nafferton Books.

Young, M. and G. Whitty (1977b), 'Perspectives on education and society', in *Society, State and Schooling*, Ringmer, The Falmer Press.

Index

185

Index